British General Elections since 1945
Second Edition

David Butler

BLACKWELL
Oxford UK & Cambridge USA

First published 1989
Reprinted 1993
Second edition 1995

Blackwell Publishers, the publishing imprint of
Basil Blackwell Ltd
108 Cowley Road, Oxford, OX4 1JF, UK

Basil Blackwell Inc.
238 Main Street
Cambridge, Massachusetts 02142, USA

British Library Cataloguing in Publication Data
A CIP catalogue record for this book is available from the British Library

Library of Congress Cataloging-in-Publication Data
Butler, David, 1924–
    British general elections since 1945/David Butler.
    p. cm. – (Making contemporary Britain)
    Includes bibliographical references and index.
    ISBN 0–631–19828–8 (pbk.)
    1. Elections – Great Britain.   2. Great Britain – Politics and government – 1945–   I. Title.   II. Series.
JN956.B869   1995   94–44010
324.941´085–dc20   CIP

Typeset in 11 on 13 pt Ehrhardt
by Joshua Associates Ltd, Oxford
Printed in Great Britain by
T. J. Press Ltd, Padstow, Cornwall
This book is printed on acid-free paper.

Contents

General Editor's Preface to the Second Edition   vii

Acknowledgements   ix

1 Continuity and Change   1

2 Fourteen General Elections   5

3 The Legal Framework   45

4 Constituencies, Seats and Votes   51

5 Franchise, Turnout and Voting Behaviour   61

6 The Timing of Elections and the Party Battle   75

7 Changing MPs   81

8 The Cost of Elections   85

9 The National Campaign   90

10 The Media   102

11 Advertising and Polls   110

12 Local Electioneering   120

13 Conclusion   122

Appendix I Election Results, 1945–1992   130

Appendix II Election Peaks and Troughs   132

Bibliography   135

Index   139

General Editor's Preface to the Second Edition

The Institute of Contemporary British History's series *Making Contemporary Britain* is aimed directly at school students, undergraduates and others interested in learning more about topics in post-war British history. In the series, authors are not attempting to break new ground, but to present clear and balanced overviews of the state of knowledge on each of the topics.

The ICBH was founded in October 1986 with the objective of promoting the study of British history since 1945 at every level. To that end it publishes books and a quarterly journal, *Contemporary Record*, it organizes seminars and conferences for school students, undergraduates, researchers and teachers of post-war history, and it runs a number of research programmes and other activities.

A central belief of the ICBH's work is that post-war history is too often neglected in British schools, institutes of higher education and beyond. The ICBH acknowledges the validity of the arguments against the study of recent history, notably the problems of bias, overly subjective teaching and writing, and the difficulties of perspective. But it believes that the values of studying post-war history outweigh the drawbacks, and that the health and future of a liberal democracy require that its citizens know more about the most recent past of their country than the limited knowledge possessed by British citizens, young and old, today. Indeed, the ICBH believes that the dangers of political indoctrination are higher when the young are *not* informed of the recent past of their country.

No one is as well qualified to write this book as Dr David

Butler. Involved as sole or co-author of every Nuffield General Election Series book since 1951, he combines insight and first-hand knowledge through having been there at the time with the skills of a detached analyst looking back over 40 years of history. It is indeed difficult to think of post-war elections without the name, and face, of David Butler coming to mind, so deeply has he identified himself with the subject.

The book blends political science with political and legal history. In the first chapter, David Butler reflects on the extensive changes that occurred between the elections of 1950 and 1992, with 1959 as a watershed. He then gives a detailed examination of each of the 14 post-war elections. He analyses the results, and discusses the principal factors responsible for voting behaviour.

The author then turns to some of the mechanics of voting. The legal framework in which elections are conducted is considered, followed by a discussion of the constituencies, which have changed markedly in size and character and have aroused periodic controversy over their boundaries since the war. In this chapter the author also discusses electoral reform and tactical voting. An examination of franchise and varying turnout in chapter 5 gives way to a study of that topic beloved by examiners, 'what influences voting behaviour'.

In the remaining chapters David Butler surveys many aspects of elections, from the timing of elections (important in the British system of variable as opposed to fixed-date elections) to election finance, the media and opinion polls.

Much has been written, especially in recent years, about individual elections, and also about voting behaviour. But no one has – in a single volume – analysed electoral change over the entire post-war period. David Butler has written such a book.

The second edition of *British General Elections since 1945* provides the opportunity for David Butler both to include new material on the general election of 1992 and to also consider recent developments in voting theory in electioneering and electoral law. It remains the most succinct and informative book on general elections.

Anthony Seldon

Acknowledgements

This short book owes everything to many generations of co-authors and research assistants and other helpers in the Nuffield series of studies of general elections, far too many to be mentioned here. But, as critical readers of this manuscript, I must explicitly thank Vernon Bogdanor, Richard Clayton, Peter Cozens, Fred Craig, Lord Fraser of Kilmorack, Anthony Heath, Anthony Seldon and Kevin Swaddle. Above all, I must acknowledge the patience of Audrey Skeats, who has typed at least ten of the Nuffield series as well as this epitome of their conclusions.

1 Continuity and Change

Democracy cannot exist without free elections, regular occasions when the people can, in an orderly fashion, throw out those who rule. Since 1945 British voters have had 14 opportunities to take power away from the party in office – and on six occasions they have done so. They have used a centuries-old voting system and a long-established legal code of conduct to carry out these civilized evictions. But, although the formal framework has remained unchanged, the past 50 years have seen a transformation in the nature and management of elections.

This short book covers the whole period of British post-war history but it is not intended as a narrative of events. What it seeks to offer is an analysis of a process, a study of how the nature of elections has been transformed by the social and technological changes of the past two generations.

Political science differs from natural science by lacking assured regularities. Similar causes do not always produce similar effects. 'No man can jump into the same river twice. Both the man and the river change.' A tactic that worked once may fail surprisingly the second time because, in some subtle way, the situation is different. The rules of the game change over the years. Although the legal regulations under which elections are conducted have continued virtually without alteration since 1945, the substance is no longer the same. Different voters, receiving different stimuli, choose different politicians for different reasons.

Consider the elections of 1950 and 1992. The 1950 contest

was fought to an overwhelming degree in the newspapers, chiefly through reports of the leaders' speeches. Television, then in its infancy, kept clear of the contest while the all-pervasive BBC radio gave it no coverage – except for 20-minute talks by five Conservative, five Labour and three Liberal spokesmen. The leaders toured the country, making major evening addresses at rallies in the big cities. Clement Attlee was driven around the provinces by his wife in their old family saloon with a detective in the back seat but no other entourage. Winston Churchill moved with more pomp by train, concentrating his appeal into half a dozen great orations. The secondary leaders made speeches too, which received extensive coverage. But at the national level there was no advertising; no regular press conferences; no serious day-to-day strategic planning by a headquarters committee. Once the manifestos had been launched, the politicians muddled through in a very individualistic way to the end.

The 1992 election offers a striking contrast. John Major, Neil Kinnock, Paddy Ashdown and David Owen would start the day with carefully planned 'photo-opportunities', go on to the morning press conferences, and then rush out of London by plane or by 'battlebus' to be seen in the provinces for a few hours; they would sometimes make an early evening speech before presenting themselves for their key television interviews. Behind all these activities stood campaign committees, pollsters and media advisers. Modern communications linked all the leading figures in each party to each other, so that a theme of the day could be established and a common reaction agreed to any new development. In this highly self-conscious projection of rival images, everything was timed, phrased and lit for the benefit of television coverage. It was all a far cry from 1950. What happened then was nearer to the campaign of 1880 than to that of 1992.

One feature of the elections of the early 1950s was that the two sides never seemed to meet. Each proceeded on its own way, explaining its own virtues and its adversary's faults but never coming to grips with the specific points put forward daily by the enemy. Each seemed to be manoeuvring on a separate battlefield against straw armies of its own devising. There were no press conferences and no broadcast confrontations or interviews at which argument could be joined and reactions compared. The early 1950s constitute the period when British elections were furthest from the image of a courtroom trial, implicit in so many newspaper editorials, where the campaign is seen as a closely reasoned quasi-judicial contest over the conduct of affairs during the past five years and the promises for the next five between prosecution (the opposition) and defence (the government) before an open-minded jury (the electorate). In fact, the argument is never conducted in a structured way and the jury come to court hopelessly compromised by a large amount of miscellaneous information and prejudice about the issues at stake – and most of them with their minds irrevocably made up.

One of the basic difficulties of writing about elections is that the campaign may to some extent be a ritual dance, a three-week repetition of well-aired themes, making no substantial net difference to the outcome. British elections are usually won over the long haul. A very large proportion of people vote out of team loyalty, supporting the party that they – and their parents too – have always supported; those who change their minds are usually converted, not during the final three weeks, but over months and years because of an accumulating impression, positive or negative, of the values and the performance of the rival parties. Yet one must not go too far in playing down the impact of campaigns. In at least two post-war elections the outcome was, almost certainly, determined by events during the three weeks of the campaign and in at least four others there was a movement of votes that transformed the margin of victory.

Elections are complex affairs, involving many people in weeks and months of intense and diverse activity, as every adult citizen is challenged to attend to a few weeks of argument before casting a ballot. 'You can no more describe a battlefield than you can describe a ballroom' said the Duke of Wellington. The same is true of elections. The purposes of this book – the study of changing electioneering – cannot be achieved by a simple narrative of each successive contest. It is necessary to divide up the electoral process into many aspects to see what has changed and what has stayed the same. But, first, it is worth offering a brief chronicle of each of the 14 post-war general elections, sufficient to remind the reader of the personalities, the salient events, the issues and the outcomes.

2 Fourteen General Elections

1945

The 1945 election was held against the background of victory in the war in Europe. On 18 May, ten days after VE day, Winston Churchill proposed that the coalition government should continue until the defeat of Japan. Although Clement Attlee and Ernest Bevin were sympathetic, the Labour party, which happened to be in Conference at Blackpool, rejected the idea. Mr Churchill then formed a 'caretaker' government, almost entirely Conservative, and asked for a dissolution on 15 June so that the election could take place on 5 July (although, to allow for delays in the postal ballots from the forces, the votes were not to be counted until 26 July).

The Labour party manifesto, *Let Us Face the Future*, attacked the Conservatives' pre-war record and promised a *Five Year Plan*, 'with a firm constructive hand on our whole productive machinery', including the nationalization of the basic industries of energy, transport and steel. The Conservatives' manifesto, *Mr Churchill's Declaration of Policy to the Electors*, was less specific, though equally vigorous in its denunciation of its opponent's capacity to manage the nation's affairs.

The election was largely conducted through nightly 20- or 30-minute radio broadcasts allotted to the parties. Four of the Conservatives' ten broadcasts were given by Mr Churchill, and the Conservative campaign revolved around his war-winning personality. One of his broadcasts, in which he suggested that socialism would mean a Gestapo for Britain, caused a major

This widely used poster underlined the extent to which the Conservative campaign in 1945 focused upon the leadership of Winston Churchill.

The *Daily Mirror* put on a very effective campaign for Labour with cartoons and headlines evoking the ills of the inter-war years. (*Daily Mirror*, June 1945)

sensation and was widely seen as counter-productive. Mr Attlee was not a frightening figure and he robustly refuted Mr Churchill's suggestion that he would be the puppet of Labour's National Executive and in particular of Professor Laski, its chairman. The *Daily Mirror* sustained a notable pro-Labour campaign on the themes 'Don't let it happen again' (i.e. war and unemployment) and 'I'll vote for him' (addressed to the wives of soldiers still serving overseas).

It was generally expected on all sides that the Conservatives would win, even though the Gallup poll since 1943 had shown a comfortable Labour lead. In fact, this lead declined during the campaign.

The result showed the biggest movement in votes recorded in any British election since 1918 (table 2.1). Compared with the previous election in 1935, there was a 12 per cent swing from Conservative to Labour and Labour jumped from 154 seats to 393. Five members of the Cabinet were defeated as well as 27 other ministers. Mr Churchill resigned at once and at 7.30 p.m. on 26 July 1945 Mr Attlee became the first Labour Prime Minister with a clear House of Commons majority. The

Table 2.1 General election of 5 July 1945

	Con	Lab	Lib	Other	Total
Seats					
At dissolution	398	166	18	33	615
After election	213	393	12	22	640
Votes					
% of total	39.8	48.3	9.1	2.8	100.0
Change since 1935 (%)	−13.9	+10.4	+2.7	+0.8	
Labour overall majority 146					
Turnout 73.3%					

MPs defeated: *Con*: L. S. Amery, B. Bracken, Sir J. Grigg, H. Macmillan, P. Thorneycroft; *Lib*: Sir W. Beveridge, Sir A. Sinclair.
MPs retiring: *Con*: Lady Astor, A. Duff Cooper; *Lab*: T. Johnston.
First full parliament for: *Con*: S. Lloyd; *Lab*: E. Bevin, G. Brown, J. Callaghan, Barbara Castle, R. Crossman, M. Foot, H. Gaitskell, H. Shawcross, M. Stewart, H. Wilson.

two minority governments of 1924 and 1929 had been short-lived; this one could last.

Labour had won not because of the campaign but because the visible success of planning and 'fair shares' during the war, together with the proven competence of Labour ministers over five years of coalition government, had already made Labour seem more appealing than the Conservatives. Many in the intellectual and middle classes were disillusioned with a party that was associated with unemployment and appeasement as well as the other real and supposed failures of the inter-war period.

1950

The Labour government, despite many post-war adversities, had fared rather well in opinion polls and had not lost a single by-election. It had seemed at one time that the parliament would run its full five years so that Labour's final nationaliza-tion promise, the takeover of the iron and steel industry, could be enacted over the House of Lords veto; but in November

Table 2.2 General election of 23 February 1950

	Con	Lab	Lib	Other	Total
Seats					
At dissolution	218	391	10	21	640
After election	299	315	9	2	625
Votes					
% of total	43.5	46.1	9.1	1.3	100.0
Change since 1945 (%)	+3.7	−2.2	+0.1	−1.4	
Labour overall majority 5					
Turnout 84%					

MPs defeated: *Lab*: A. Creech Jones, Sir F. Soskice; *Ind. Lab*: D. N. Pritt, K. Zilliacus; *Comm*: W. Gallagher; *Lib*: G. Lloyd George.
MPs retiring: *Lab*: L. Silkin; *Nat*: Sir J. Anderson; *Ind*: Sir A. Herbert.
First full parliament for: *Con*: E. Heath, R. Maudling, I. Macleod, E. Powell, C. Soames; *Lab*: A. Crosland, R. Jenkins; *Lib*: J. Grimond.

THE TWENTY-THIRD MAN

The 1950 campaign was seen as a straightforward challenge to the Labour government by Churchill and the Conservatives, but the Liberal party, led by Clement Davies, putting up 475 candiates, confused the issue. (*Daily Mail*, February 1950)

1949 a compromise clause, delaying implementation until after an election, cleared the decks. The election was announced on 11 January for 23 February, the first contest early in the year since January 1910. The Labour party manifesto, *Let Us Win Through Together*, asked for a mandate to nationalize sugar, cement and industrial assurance, but it was in general cautious, dominated by Herbert Morrison's slogan of 'consolidation'. The Conservatives' manifesto, *This is the Road*, was the product of their high-powered research department which had led the party to a new stance. Although the document promised to stop and, if possible, reverse the process of nationalization and to end socialist waste and bureaucracy, it did completely accept the newly enacted welfare state legislation and promised to maintain full employment. Tate and Lyle ran a controversial 'Mr Cube' advertising drive against sugar nationalization, but the main election campaign lacked great events. The most colourful occurrence was an earthy broadcast attack on the Labour party by Dr Charles Hill, but the most notable was a call by Mr Churchill for a Summit meeting.

Because of the redrawing of boundaries, Labour was bound to lose seats (19 of the 62 constituencies in the heavily Labour London County Council area disappeared altogether), but the narrow outcome – a five-seat majority for Labour – was a surprise (table 2.2). A total of 319 of the 475 Liberals lost their deposits. Labour, although 2.6 per cent ahead in votes, was left with an uncertain mandate.

1951

In March 1950 it had not been clear whether Labour could survive with a majority of only five seats. But, despite a Conservative 'harrying' campaign led by Robert Boothby, there were no parliamentary troubles. The Korean War in the summer of 1950 diverted economic recovery into rearmament. The Labour government lost the key figures of Bevin and Cripps (through illness and death) and Bevan and Wilson (through resignation). Clement Attlee abruptly and without consultation asked for a dissolution on 19 September, 1951 while an international crisis was in progress, caused by the expulsion of the British from the Abadan oil fields by Dr Mussadiq, the Prime Minister of Iran.

Labour entered the election well behind in the opinion polls but its candidates played vigorously on fears that a Conservative return would lead to unemployment, to a dismantling of the welfare state, and even to war. The *Daily Mirror* election-day headline 'Whose finger on the trigger?' led to a successful libel action by Mr Churchill. The Conservatives attributed much of the swing back to Labour during the campaign to the 'warmonger' scare, exploited at the grass roots in Labour leaflets and speeches.

The campaign echoed 1950 except that the Liberals, with

Daily Mirror THURS OCT. 25 1951
1½d
No. 14,915
FORWARD WITH THE PEOPLE
Registered at G.P.O. as a Newspaper.

WHOSE FINGER?

BIG ISSUES OF 1951

Today YOUR finger is on the trigger

SEE YOU DEFEND

PEACE with SECURITY and PROGRESS with FAIR SHARES

VOTE FOR THE PARTY YOU CAN REALLY TRUST

The 'Daily Mirror' believes that Party is Labour

Fears that a Conservative victory would increase the risk of war were exploited by some Labour leaders and candidates during the campaign. The warmonger theme was most explicitly portrayed by the *Daily Mirror* on their election-day front page. Winston Churchill successfully sued the paper for libel. (*Daily Mirror*, 25 October 1951)

Table 2.3 General election of 25 October 1951

	Con	Lab	Lib	Other	Total
Seats					
At dissolution	298	314	9	4	625
After election	321	295	6	3	625
Votes					
% of total	48.0	48.8	2.5	0.7	100.0
Change since 1950 (%)	+4.5	+2.4	−6.6	−0.3	
Conservative overall majority 17					
Turnout 82.5%					

MPs defeated: *Lib*: Lady M. Lloyd George.
MPs retiring: *Con*: D. Clifton Brown.
First full parliament for: *Con*: Sir E. Boyle, A. Barber; *Lab*: T. Benn.

only 109 candidates, were no longer a significant force. The Conservatives in their pragmatic manifesto, *Britain Strong and Free*, took advantage of Aneurin Bevan's resignation and the radical utterances of his supporters to paint a lurid picture of the dangerous forces behind the mild Clement Attlee. Against the continuing appeal of Labour's 'fair shares', the Conservatives could play on the weariness wth post-war austerities.

The election was notable for the first party broadcasts on television, even though the 15-minute appearances – one for each party – were fairly anodyne and were seen by relatively few voters.

On the evening of 25 October it was plain that Labour had lost ground but the Conservative victory in seats was not certain until the following afternoon (table 2.3). Mr Attlee immediately resigned and Churchill returned to No. 10 Downing St. Labour, in fact, won more votes than the Conservatives; its total, 13,950,000, representing the largest number of votes ever cast for a single party in a British general election.

1955

Between 1951 and 1955 prosperity grew slowly and rationing ended. The Korean War was concluded. Stalin died. The Coronation in 1953 and the conquest of Everest seemed to mark a change in national mood. The government fared relatively well in by-elections and opinion polls and built up a solid record of moderately non-contentious achievement.

On 6 April 1955 Sir Winston Churchill resigned the premiership and Sir Anthony Eden was sworn in as his successor. On 15 April he asked the Queen to dissolve the three and a half year old parliament on 6 May. A buoyant, some would say an electioneering, budget was rushed through. The election, the last to be left uncovered by the broadcasters, was a tranquil affair, the least memorable of all the post-war contests. The Conservative policy statement, *United for Peace and Progress*, made fewer specific promises than any post-war manifesto. Labour's *Forward with Labour* contained commitments to restore a totally free health service and to abolish the 11–plus examination but it too was modest in scope. The flatness became especially evident after the Gallup poll settled down to

Table 2.4 General election of 26 May 1955

	Con	Lab	Lib	Other	Total
Seats					
At dissolution	322	294	6	3	625
After election	345	277	6	2	630
Votes					
% of total	49.7	46.4	2.7	1.2	100.0
Change since 1951 (%)	+1.7	−2.4	+0.2	+0.5	

Conservative overall majority 54

Turnout 76.8%

MPs defeated: *Lab*: A. Crosland, M. Foot, W. Wyatt.
MPs retiring: *Con*: R. Assheton; *Lab*: J. Freeman.
First full parliament for: *Con*: W. Whitelaw; *Lab*: D. Healey, R. Mason.

Aneurin Bevan resigned in April 1951. Thereafter the Conservative press in the 1951 election and still more in the 1955 election exploited the wild suggestion that the Bevanites would take over the Labour party and that Attlee was merely a stalking horse for Bevan. (*Daily Express*, May 1955)

record a comfortable 4 per cent lead for the government. Labour, still led by the ageing Clement Attlee, promised some further nationalization but the party was handicapped not only by the continued rumblings of the Bevanite split (Bevan had lost the whip and narrowly avoided expulsion from the party a month earlier) but also by the fact that its themes of 1951 (that the Conservatives would bring war, unemployment and a dismantling of the social services) had been shown to be false by events. There was, however, no serious third party challenge and Labour held on to the overwhelming bulk of their traditional vote and even picked up one Norfolk seat against the tide. But, for the first time since 1949, a government was able to face parliament with a comfortable majority and, for the first time in 90 years, the party that had been in power improved on its performance in the previous election (table 2.4).

1959

The Conservatives had a rougher ride in 1955–9 than in the previous parliament. Sir Anthony Eden showed limited command when the economy slumped in 1955–6. After the seizure of the Suez Canal in July 1956, he led the country into the ill-fated Anglo-French intervention of October. His health collapsed and, from January 1957, Harold Macmillan presided insouciantly over a substantial economic recovery. He brushed off the resignation in 1957 of Lord Salisbury over colonial policy and, a year later, of the Chancellor of the Exchequer, Peter Thorneycroft, over economic restraint. The ending of military conscription was announced and the first motorway was opened. Labour gained three seats from the Conservatives in by-elections in 1957–8 (and the Liberals one). The Campaign for Nuclear Disarmament started its Aldermaston marches in 1957, but Hugh Gaitskell, Labour's new leader, patched up his differences with Aneurin Bevan, the Shadow Foreign Secretary, and the Labour party entered the 1959 election in better heart than for many years, believing that they had a real chance of victory. Their manifesto, *Britain Belongs to You*,

'Well, gentlemen, I think we all fought a good fight . . .'

Before the 1959 election the Conservative advertising campaign 'Life's better with the Conservatives' focused onthe growing prosperity of Britain symbolized by the ever-widening sale of consumer durables. Macmillan's record victory was seen as the reward.

promised the municipalization of rented accommodation, an increase in pensions and a full national superannuation scheme. The Conservatives, in *The Next Five Years*, boasted of their achievements and, in a list of modest proposals, promised a Ministry of Science and special measures to combat unemployment black-spots.

The Conservatives were 7 per cent ahead in the polls when Mr Macmillan called the election on 8 September 1959 for 8 October, the earliest possible autumn date. The parliament had lasted four and a half years. The election was more exciting than its predecessors. There were more opinion polls and they plainly showed a slump in government support as the campaign advanced. If this were to continue to the end, a Labour victory seemed possible. But the Conservatives, who had built up support earlier in the year with a notable advertising campaign beginning 'Life's better with the Conservatives' and capped by 'Don't let Labour ruin it', rallied in the last ten days. Labour's adroit innovations – in Morgan Phillips' daily press conferences and in the party election broadcasts – were belatedly matched by the Conservatives. And Mr Gaitskell

Table 2.5 General election of 8 October 1959

	Con	Lab	Lib	Other	Total
Seats					
At dissolution	342	281	6	1	630
After election	365	258	6	1	630
Votes					
% of total	49.4	43.8	5.9	0.9	100.0
Change since 1955 (%)	−0.3	−2.6	+3.2	−0.2	
Conservative overall majority 100					
Turnout 78.7%					

MPs defeated: *Lab*: A. Bottomley, I. Mikardo; *Lib*: M. Bonham-Carter.
MPs retiring: *Con*: W. S. Morrison, J. Stuart; *Lab*: H. Dalton, H. Morrison, T. Williams.
First full parliament for: *Con*: Margaret Thatcher, Sir K. Joseph, J. Prior, N. Ridley; *Lab*: Judith Hart; *Lib*: J. Thorpe.

made a campaign blunder. In reply to the Conservative gibe 'Where's the money coming from?', he gave a doubt-raising pledge: 'There will be no increase in ... income tax so long as normal peacetime conditions continue.' At the same time a Labour handout promised a reduction in purchase tax. There is little doubt that this seriously damaged the credibility of the Labour campaign, which Mr Gaitskell's personality, 'the man with a plan', and the Labour commitment to growth had done much to enhance. The Liberals, under an enthusiastic new Leader, Jo Grimond, fought on a much wider scale but, as so often happens, were squeezed by the dominance of a two-party battle.

The Conservative campaign was encapsulated in Mr Macmillan's much-quoted remark to a factory worker, 'You've never had it so good', and in the end prosperity won the day. It was plain from the first results that the Conservatives had won – and with an increased majority (table 2.5). With less than 200 constituencies declared, Mr Gaitskell made history by conceding defeat in a television interview. No party since the Great Reform Bill had won three full parliamentary terms in a row and Mr Macmillan, who had come to office at a low point less than three years before, was hailed as 'Supermac'.

1964

The Conservative triumph of 1959 continued till mid-1961. The Labour party, after their disappointment, fell into disarray, quarrelling first over their 'Clause Four' commitment to public ownership and then over nuclear weapons. But in 1961 the scene changed. The economy faltered. The first attempt to enter the European Community was launched. Selwyn Lloyd's 'pay pause' was introduced to check inflation and the corporatist institutions, 'Neddy', the National Economic Development Office, and 'Nicky', the National Incomes Commission, were set up. The government grew increasingly unpopular. In March 1962 the Conservative stronghold of Orpington was lost to the Liberals and three more Conservative seats fell to Labour before the year was out. On 14 July

Table 2.6 General election of 15 October 1964

	Con	Lab	Lib	Other	Total
Seats					
At dissolution	360	261	7	2	630
After election	304	317	9	–	630
Votes					
% of total	43.4	44.1	11.2	1.3	100.0
Change since 1959 (%)	−6.0	+0.3	+5.3	+0.4	
Labour overall majority 5					
Turnout 77.1%					

MPs defeated: *Con*: R. Bevins, A. Barber; *Lab*: P. Gordon Walker, F. Brockway.
MPs retiring: *Con*: Sir W. Churchill, H. Macmillan; *Lab*: A. Creech-Jones, J. Chuter Ede.
First full parliament for: *Con*: J. Biffen, G. Howe, F. Pym, P. Walker, G. Younger; *Lab*: R. Hattersley, M. Rees, J. Silkin, P. Shore, Shirley Williams.

"BUT THINGS MIGHT START SLIPPING IN THE LAST FEW DAYS . . . THEY WON'T SLIP TOWARDS US."—Mr. R. A. Butler in a Daily Express interview today.

The Labour party was plainly favourite to win the 1964 general election. R. A. Butler, denied the premiership by Sir Alec Douglas-Home, gave an indiscreet interview on a train journey four days before the end of the campaign. (*Evening Standard*, 9 October 1964)

1962, in 'the night of long knives', Mr Macmillan abruptly dismissed seven members of his Cabinet. In January 1963 President de Gaulle snubbed Britain's application for European membership. In the same month, Hugh Gaitskell died, to be succeeded by the thrusting but essentially tactical Harold Wilson. In June 1963 the Profumo scandal broke and Mr Macmillan's position became even more insecure until, in October, ill health finally provoked his resignation. He was unexpectedly succeeded by the Earl of Home (who was able to renounce his peerage because of legislation just passed in response to Tony Benn's campaign to avoid inheriting the title of Lord Stansgate). The fact that Sir Alec Douglas-Home was preferred to R. A. Butler led to Iain Macleod and Enoch Powell deserting the Cabinet. But under the new Prime Minister the Conservatives steadied despite a divisive row over the abolition of Resale Price Maintenance. The election was, however, put off until the last moment. It was the first peacetime parliament to run its full term since 1722.

Prosperity with a Purpose, the Conservative manifesto, suffered from the difficulties of a long-standing incumbent government which had been going through a bad patch. Labour's, *The New Britain*, with its emphasis on purposive planning and its attacks on the 'stop-go' policies of the preceding few years, stands out as perhaps the most confident and optimistic of these post-war documents.

The campaign was more lively than any subsequent one has been. Sir Alec Douglas-Home was shouted down in Birmingham and elsewhere, as he gallantly insisted on his own issue of nuclear defence against Harold Wilson's 'white heat of the technological revolution'.

The exuberance of George Brown for Labour and Quintin Hogg for the Conservatives gave ammunition to their opponents. Strikes at Hardy Spicers and at British Oxygen were seen as 'politically motivated' embarrassments to Labour. Encouraged by Orpington, the Liberals put on their most significant campaign since 1950.

The opinion polls fluctuated during the campaign but a Labour victory was generally expected. The swing was the largest since 1945 but it was only enough to give them a clear

"HA-HA, OLD WILSON'S IN AN AWFUL DILEMMA!"

Harold Wilson, with a five-seat majority, reduced still further by the Leyton by-election, could plainly not put off a dissolution indefinitely. There was much speculation about the date, but Labour's prospects were always better than those of the Conservatives under their new leader, Edward Heath. (*Evening Standard*, 8 February 1966)

"Marvellous! My popularity among the passengers isn't sinking!"

Labour's economic team, Wilson, Brown and Callaghan, faced great balance of payments difficulties, but Labour entered the 1966 election ahead in the opinion polls. (*Daily Express*, 11 March 1966)

majority of five seats (table 2.6). The Conservatives actually made a few gains against the tide, including Smethwick, where Labour's intended Foreign Secretary, Patrick Gordon-Walker, was defeated after a racialist campaign, but the Liberals picked up three Conservative seats in the north of Scotland. Labour's return to office after 13 years in the wilderness had an uncertain quality to it.

1966

The 1964–6 parliament showed Harold Wilson at his most ingenious, as he manoeuvred for a more workable majority. The by-election defeat at Leyton of his new Foreign Secretary, Patrick Gordon-Walker, cut Labour's majority to three seats. Major legislation was impossible but much effort went into a National Plan devised by George Brown at the new Department of Economic Affairs.

Sir Alec Douglas-Home gave up the Conservative leadership in July 1965 and Edward Heath narrowly defeated Reginald Maudling for the succession.

Table 2.7 General election of 31 March 1966

	Con	*Lab*	*Lib*	*Other*	*Total*
Seats					
At dissolution	304	316	10	–	630
After election	253	363	12	2	630
Votes					
% of total	41.9	47.9	8.5	1.7	100.0
Change since 1964 (%)	−1.5	+3.8	−2.7	+0.4	
Labour overall majority 96					
Turnout 75.8%					

MPs defeated: *Con*: C. Soames, P. Thorneycroft, H. Brooke, M. Redmayne, G. Howe; *Lib*: R. Bowen.
MPs retiring: *Lab*: Sir F. Soskice, J. Griffiths.
First full parliament for: *Con*: M. Heseltine; *Lab*: D. Owen; *Lib*: D. Steel, J. Pardoe.

Labour fared well in the opinion polls and, after a notable by-election success in Hull in January 1966, Mr Wilson decided that it was safe to go to the country again. The campaign was one-sided, and affected by the general assumption that Labour would win easily. There were no surprises or major new issues. *Time for Decision* echoed the themes of Labour's 1964 manifesto, while the Conservatives' *Action not Words* moved more strongly than before towards endorsing

From 1968 onwards, after his 'rivers of blood' speech, Enoch Powell and his stance on immigration were a constant problem for the Conservatives, and at the height of the 1970 election there was great pressure to repudiate him as a Conservative candidate. Edward Heath stood firm and in the end Enoch Powell asked all his supporters to vote Conservative. (*Tribune*, 26 April 1968)

entry into Europe and trade union reform. Edward Heath attacked Labour with the slogans 9–5–1 (9 per cent wage increases, 5 per cent inflation, 1 per cent growth) and 'vote now, pay later'. But those who were enjoying 9 per cent wage increases were not necessarily impressed by the dangers implied. Labour offered nothing beyond the 1964 manifesto but asked for the majority to carry it out. Mr Heath campaigned doggedly but Mr Wilson's faster footwork was rewarded by a clear majority of 96, the party's only comfortable victory apart from 1945 (table 2.7).

1970

On 20 July, three months after the 1966 election, the Labour government was forced to make drastic economic cuts to stop a run on the pound and these effectively put an end to George Brown's National Plan. After the devaluation crisis of 1967 and General de Gaulle's 'No' to Britain's second attempt to enter the Common Market, the government suffered heavily in the opinion polls, in local elections and in by-elections. It faced difficulties from demonstrations against the Vietnam War and the beginnings of the Northern Ireland troubles, and was humiliated by its own side in its 'In Place of Strife' attempt at trade union reform. The Conservatives, despite low poll ratings for Mr Heath and a major row over Enoch Powell's 'anti-immigration' speech in April 1968, seemed assured of a return to power. But in late 1969, as the balance of payments turned round, Labour recovered, and when the party moved into the lead in the polls in April 1970 Mr Wilson decided to dissolve the four-year-old parliament for an election on 18 June.

In halcyon summer weather, everything went well for the government with its manifesto slogan *Now Britain's Strong — Let's Make Her Great to Live in*, while Mr Heath's elaborate programmes set out in *A Better Tomorrow* seemed to make little impact despite some innovative Conservative television presentations. Labour's re-election appeared assured until the spell was broken two days before the vote by adverse balance of payments figures for May. Other factors conspired to change

Harold Wilson, in his efforts to make the Labour party the national party of government, was seen in 1970 as having moved further and further from socialism. (*Punch*, 20 May 1970)

the mood: England was knocked out of the World Cup, the controversial Enoch Powell urged his followers to vote Conservative, and some sharp price rises were announced.

There was a last-minute swing (which only one opinion poll picked up). Labour voters may have abstained (the turnout was the lowest since 1935). In defiance of predictions, Edward Heath won a clear majority of 30 on a 4.7 per cent swing, the largest recorded since 1945. Labour was punished for four

Table 2.8 General election of 18 June 1970

	Con	*Lab*	*Lib*	*Other*	*Total*
Seats					
At dissolution	264	346	13	7	630
After election	330	287	6	7	630
Votes					
% of total	46.4	43.0	7.5	3.1	100.0
Change since 1966 (%)	+4.5	−4.9	−1.0	+1.4	
Conservative overall majority 30					
Turnout 72.0%					

MPs defeated: *Con*: K. Baker; *Lab*: G. Brown, J. Diamond, Sir D. Foot, J. Lee; *Lib*: E. Lubbock; *PC*: G. Evans; *S. Nat*: Winnie Ewing.
MPs retiring: *Con*: Sir E. Boyle; *Lab*: E. Shinwell.
First full parliament for: *Con*: K. Clarke, N. Tebbit; *Lab*: G. Kaufman, N. Kinnock, J. Prescott, J. Smith; *SNP*: D. Stewart; *Dem. Unionists*: I. Paisley.

years of economic uncertainty. Mr Wilson's triumph in the belated recovery of the balance of payments was nullified by the freak May figures. The Conservatives' victory was the reward for being an acceptable alternative to a government that had been through troubled times.

February 1974

Mr Heath's government had one major achievement: entry into the European Community on 1 January 1973. But otherwise it fared ill. Its far-reaching Industrial Relations Act of 1971 alienated the trade unions and failed to operate effectively. The government was humiliated by the miners in a 1972 strike. In Northern Ireland it was forced to impose direct rule. Its economic policies did not succeed in containing inflation or in correcting the adverse balance of payments. The Cabinet indulged in minor U-turns on policy with the crisis national-ization in 1971 of Rolls-Royce and Upper Clyde Shipbuilders

During the hurried crisis election of February 1974, Enoch Powell, who had refused to stand as a Conservative, advised electors to vote Labour as the only way to get Britain out of the European Community. (*Sunday Express*, 1974)

Table 2.9 General election of 28 February 1974

	Con	Lab	Lib	Other	Total
Seats					
At dissolution	323	287	11	9	630
After election	297	301	14	23	635
Votes					
% of total	37.9	37.1	19.3	5.7	100.0
Change since 1970 (%)	−8.5	−5.9	+11.8	+2.6	

Labour overall majority *minus* 34

Turnout 78.1%

MPs defeated: *Con*: G. Campbell, N. Scott; *Lab*: J. Mackintosh.
MPs retiring: *Con*: E. Powell, D. Sandys, E. Marples; *Lab*: R. Crossman, P. Gordon-Walker, T. Driberg.
First full parliament for: *Con*: K. Baker, L. Brittan, D. Hurd, N. Lawson, J. Moore, N. Lamont, C. Parkinson, M. Rifkind; *Lab*: R. Cook; *Lib*: A. Beith, C. Smith; *PC*: D. E. Thomas.

and on a grand scale in 1972 when it decided to impose an incomes policy.

The Labour party was, however, divided by the issue of entry into the European Community and its performance in opposition was ineffective. The Liberals gained four seats in by-elections in 1972–3, the Scottish Nationalists one and Labour none. In late 1973, following the Arab–Israeli war, the price of oil quadrupled and, at the same time, the miners challenged the government's pay policy. The government declared a three-day working week to avert a fuel crisis (which had been produced by the Yom Kippur War as well as by the coal shortage). Edward Heath called an emergency election to take place on 28 February over the issue 'who governs?'

The Conservatives fought on the manifesto slogan *Firm Action for a Fair Britain* in contrast to Labour's *Let Us Work Together*, with their appeal *You Can Change the Face of Britain*. This shortest of post-war campaigns saw a remarkable 'plague on both your houses' upsurge for the Liberals who in three weeks jumped from 7 to 20 per cent in the opinion polls, as well as for the Scottish and Welsh Nationalists. The Conservatives mishandled the campaign, especially when the pay commission under Sir Frank Figgures unexpectedly seemed to imply that the miners were probably underpaid rather than overpaid. Enoch Powell refused to stand as a Conservative and, in a spectacular campaign intervention, advised voters to support Labour in order to get the country out of the Common Market.

Labour's quiet campaign may not have won many votes but Jeremy Thorpe's appeal for moderation drew away significant Conservative support. A Conservative victory was, nevertheless, generally expected and they did indeed win most votes. But Labour with only 37 per cent won 301 seats, four more than the Conservatives with 38 per cent (table 2.9). The Liberals with 14 MPs, the Nationalists with nine, and the assorted Ulstermen with 12, held the balance of power in the first inconclusive election result since 1929. Edward Heath did not resign at once but, after four days, when it was plain that he could not secure Liberal support, he gave way to Harold Wilson.

This, the first crisis election since 1931, showed how difficult it is for a government to sustain one theme for three weeks. Mr Heath's administration, the only one-term government since 1929, lost because other issues from a troubled three years came up during the campaign and because of Conservative clumsiness in sustaining the presentation of their central theme.

October 1974

Despite the indeterminate result of the February 1974 election, no party wanted an immediate dissolution. Harold Wilson's government was not seriously challenged in parliament until it was too late to call a summer election. But a great deal happened. The miners' dispute was settled, largely on the strikers' terms. The Conservative pay policy and their union legislation was repealed. The somewhat spurious 're-negotiation' of British membership of the European Community was begun. The power-sharing executive in Northern Ireland was brought down by a strike of Protestant workers.

" Well, I still think it's designed for more than one . . ."

Edward Heath's main campaign ploy in October 1974 was to call for a 'government of national unity'. (*Guardian*, 12 October 1974)

Table 2.10 General election of 10 October 1974

	Con	Lab	Lib	Other	Total
Seats					
At dissolution	297	300	15	23	635
After election	277	319	13	26	635
Votes					
% of total	35.8	39.2	18.3	6.7	100.0
Change since					
Feb. 1974 (%)	−2.1	+2.1	−1.0	+1.0	
Labour overall majority 3					
Turnout 72.8%					

MPs defeated: *Lib*: C. Mayhew; *Ind*: E. Milne, D. Taverne.
MPs retiring: *Con*: A. Barber, Sir A. Douglas-Home.
First full parliament for: *Lab*: B. Gould, Mrs M. Beckett; *PC*: G. Evans.

Labour nevertheless moved ahead in the opinion polls and Gallup was recording an 8 per cent lead for them when on 18 September Harold Wilson called an election for 10 October. The Conservatives had been somewhat shell-shocked by their defeat in February and Mr Heath was given little chance of regaining power. Just before the campaign Sir Keith Joseph had repudiated the record of Conservative government and condemned all incomes policies. The Labour party with its manifesto, *Britain Will Win*, made much of Conservative divisions, while the Conservatives in *Putting Britain First* pointed to galloping inflation.

But, during the brief and relatively quiet campaign, the most notable event was a 'non-negotiable' promise by Margaret Thatcher to cut mortgages to 9.5 per cent by Christmas; this was shown by surveys to have dented the party's credibility. Two weeks before the vote Edward Heath, who tried to obliterate the memories of the previous winter's confrontation with a low key emollient approach, proposed a government of national unity, but could not bring himself to offer the 'supreme sacrifice' of his own position.

The Conservative campaign may have had some impact, for the polls greatly overpredicted a Labour victory. The promised landslide turned into a clear majority of just three seats as Labour made only 20 net gains over February (table 2.10). The Scottish Nationalists went up from seven to 11 MPs while, for once, the Liberals made no advance as the campaign progressed. As in 1966, Mr Wilson had used a short parliament to lever himself to a better position but this time he failed to achieve an effective working majority.

1979

Despite a majority of only three (which had disappeared by April 1976), the Labour government survived for four and a half years. It faced many vicissitudes: deep divisions over European membership (only partially resolved by the 1975 referendum which by a two to one majority backed staying in the EEC); sharp inflation; a balance of payments crisis that led to an IMF visitation in 1976 and sharp cut-backs in public spending; much travail over Scottish and Welsh devolution; an uncertain pact with the Liberals in 1977–8; and finally a disastrous collision with the unions over incomes policy.

The government faced some appalling poll findings and by-election reverses in mid-parliament, but by the late summer of 1978 it looked as though Labour had a chance of winning re-election in the autumn. However, Mr Callaghan (who had succeeded Mr Wilson in April 1976) surprised everyone by postponing the dissolution until 1979. The 'winter of discontent' followed, with the Labour party suffering from much-publicized industrial action against its pay policy, notably by hospital porters and gravediggers. The government's unpopularity led to the defeat of the Scottish devolution referendum on 1 March 1979 and hence to the hostility of the Scottish Nationalists; they joined with the Liberals and Conservatives in support of a no-confidence motion which was carried by 311 to 310 on 23 March. The election could not be held until 3 May and the government continued on a caretaker basis till then.

"If you must have a Conservative
Prime Minister, I'm your man."

Jim Callaghan fought the 1979 election on a moderate platform, to the
annoyance of many Labour activists. (*Sunday Mirror*, 8 April 1979)

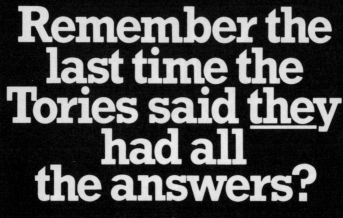

Remember the last time the Tories said <u>they</u> had all the answers?

Keep Britain Labour.

Labour, struggling after the 'winter of discontent', tried in its advertising to evoke memories of the three-day week imposed by Edward Health in 1973–4.

Table 2.11 General election of 3 May 1979

	Con	Lab	Lib	Other	Total
Seats					
At dissolution	284	309	14	28	635
After election	339	269	11	16	635
Votes					
% of total	43.9	36.9	13.8	5.4	100.0
Change since 1974 (%)	+8.1	−2.3	−4.5	−1.3	
Conservative overall majority 43					
Turnout 76.0%					

MPs defeated: *Con*: E. Taylor; *Lab*: B. Gould, Shirley Williams; *Lib*: E. Hooson,
   J. Pardoe, J. Thorpe; *PC*: G. Evans; *SNP*: Winifred Ewing.
MPs retiring: *Lab*: Barbara Castle, E. Dell, W. Ross, M. Stewart, G. Strauss.
First full parliament for: *Con*: J. Major, C. Patten, J. Patten, W. Waldegrave.

The Conservatives had changed considerably during the 1974–9 parliament. Despite his second defeat, Mr Heath tried to carry on as leader. Mrs Thatcher announced that she would stand against him, and in February 1975 she prevailed, first against Mr Heath, and then against William Whitelaw, to become the first woman leader of a major British party.

The 1979 election was conducted in the expectation of a Conservative victory – they started 10 per cent ahead in the polls. Mrs Thatcher's manifesto, unadventurously titled *The Conservative Manifesto 1979*, promised strict control of the money supply and a reduction in public spending; compulsory balloting in unions and firm action against secondary picketing and closed shops; a hands-off policy towards pay settlements; and a limited amount of denationalization. Labour, in its manifesto *The Labour Way Is the Better Way*, did not offer new policies but challenged the Conservatives to say where the money would come from for their tax cuts. The Liberals fought under a new leader, David Steel, who had taken over in 1976 when Jeremy Thorpe had to depart under a cloud; the Conservative–Labour battle meant, however, that the Liberals were pushed more to the sidelines than in 1974 and, like the Scottish Nationalists, they fell back significantly. The government recovered some votes but the Conservatives were too far ahead; neither they nor their leader blundered during the campaign and at 2.30 p.m. on 4 May Mr Callaghan resigned; an hour later, Mrs Thatcher, with a clear majority of 43, became Britain's first woman Prime Minister (table 2.11).

1983

Mrs Thatcher's government had an uneasy start. Inflation soared (helped by a doubling of VAT in the June 1979 budget) and so did unemployment. The pure monetarist theories did not seem to work and there was open hostility to Mrs Thatcher's more right-wing policies from some members of the Cabinet. However, the Labour party encountered even worse troubles as it repudiated much of the policy of the 1974–9

"Not everyone wants me to quit. Kind Mrs Thatcher wants me to stay!"

From the start of the 1983 campaign the Labour party, and more particularly their leader, Michael Foot, who travelled with his dog, Disraeli, were seen to be faring disastrously. (*Daily Express*, 3 June 1983)

government and the parliamentary party chose Michael Foot as successor to Jim Callaghan. Mr Foot's leadership failed to unite the party and he received poor ratings in the polls. In January 1981 Roy Jenkins and three other former Cabinet ministers, together with over 20 MPs, broke away to form the Social Democratic Party which quickly formed an Alliance with the Liberals. The centre parties prospered and, after Shirley Williams's November 1981 by-election victory in the Conservative stronghold of Crosby, the Alliance even touched 50 per cent in the opinion polls. But the economy was beginning to turn around, helped perhaps by Mrs Thatcher's insistence on unexpectedly tough budgetary measures, and by March 1982 the three parties were on level terms in the opinion polls. Then the Falklands War transformed the scene. By the time the Falkland Islands were recaptured in June 1982 the Conservatives had soared to a comfortable lead which they sustained for some years.

The Labour party continued to shed support and in February 1983 lost the safe seat of Bermondsey to the Liberals. David Steel and Roy Jenkins maintained the Alliance as serious challengers but when, on 9 May, Margaret Thatcher announced an election for 9 June, she could feel confident of

Table 2.12 General election of 9 June 1983

	Con	Lab	Lib	Other	Total
Seats					
At dissolution	336	240	42	17	635
After election	397	209	23	21	650
Votes					
% of total	42.4	27.6	25.4	4.6	100.0
Change since 1979 (%)	−1.5	−9.3	+11.6	−0.8	

Conservative overall majority 144

Turnout 72.7%

MPs defeated: *Lab*: T. Benn; *SDP*: Shirley Williams, W. Rodgers; *Ind*: G. Fitt.
MPs retiring: *Lab*: Sir H. Wilson; *Lib*: J Grimond.
First full parliament for: *Con*: M. Howard; *Lab*: G. Brown; *Lib*: P. Ashdown.

victory. Unemployment was at a record level but inflation had tapered off and prosperity was visibly growing.

Labour's manifesto, *New Hope for Britain*, was described by one Shadow Cabinet member as 'the longest suicide note in history'. It promised to leave the European Community and to adopt a non-nuclear defence policy. It also proposed large increases in public expenditure, further nationalization and central planning. It committed the party to cutting unemployment to one million within five years.

The Alliance in *Working Together for Britain* also promised to cut unemployment (by one million in two years) and to use government resources to further investment. But it was a conciliatory document. The government's appeal, *The Conservative Manifesto 1983*, pointed with pride to the government's achievements; its main new proposals were the privatization of British Telecom, British Airways, British Steel and other industries, as well as the abolition of the Greater London Council and the six Metropolitan Authorities.

The campaign was mainly notable for the upsurge of the Alliance whose support rose from 14 to 26 per cent in the last 14 days; they almost overtook Labour, despite internal crises about whether David Steel should supplant Roy Jenkins at the head of the Alliance. In the end the Alliance secured only 23 seats while Labour, a mere 2 per cent ahead in votes, won 209 (table 2.12). Labour's 28 per cent of the vote was its lowest percentage since 1918; Michael Foot's leadership, and the manifesto promises to abandon nuclear weapons and to leave Europe, were given the blame.

But the Conservatives had won not just because of the division of their opponents; for part at least of the population their policies seemed to have brought prosperity, and the Falklands' triumph had underlined the smack of firm leadership which Mrs Thatcher offered.

1987

Mrs Thatcher's second term ran more smoothly than her first. Her industrial relations legislation and policy were tested by

"Well it was never till death us do part!"

During the 1987 campaign the twin-headed Alliance failed to make the advance that the 1983 campaign had led them to expect. It was increasingly felt that David Owen's sympathies were closer to Margaret Thatcher and David Steel's to Neil Kinnock. (*The Times*, 5 June 1987)

the prolonged but unsuccessful miners' strike in 1984–5 and by the printers' dispute in Wapping in 1985–6. The worst moment for the government came with the Westland Affair. In January 1986 Michael Heseltine and later Leon Brittan resigned from the Cabinet during a row over the sale of the helicopter firm. In all, the government lost three by-elections to the Alliance and one to Labour. But when Margaret Thatcher sought the dissolution of a four-year-old parliament the Conservatives entered the contest as firm favourites. Inflation had stayed in the 4–5 per cent range. Unemployment had fallen. The pound was strong and the economy was growing. Neil Kinnock, who succeeded Michael Foot as Labour party leader in September 1983, had done much to put the party's house in order but it still had fundamental problems and it

Table 2.13 General election of 11 June 1987

	Con	Lab	Lib	Other	Total
Seats					
At dissolution	393	208	27	22	650
After election	376	229	22	23	650
Votes					
% of total	42.2	30.8	22.6	4.4	100.0
Change since 1983 (%)	−0.2	+3.2	−2.8	−0.2	
Conservative overall majority 102					
Turnout 75.3%					

MPs defeated: *Alln*: R. Jenkins, C. Freud; *UU*: E. Powell; *SNP*: G. Wilson.
MPs retiring: *Con*: Sir K. Joseph, J. Prior, F. Pym, N. St John Stevas; *Lab*: Sir J.
   Callaghan, I. Mikardo; *Lib*: R. Wainwright; *SNP*: D. Stewart.
First full parliament for *Con*: Mrs V. Bottomley, M. Portillo.

entered the summer 1987 contest while still recovering from its humiliation by the SDP in the Greenwich by-election in February.

The Conservatives echoed their 1964 manifesto slogan with *The Next Moves Forward*, while Labour reverted to their October 1974 title *Britain Will Win*; the Alliance theme was *Britain United*.

The campaign was notable for the slickness of much of the Labour effort, especially for a brilliant broadcast boosting Neil Kinnock; for an unprecedented amount of press advertising, mainly by the Conservatives; for the growing unease of the Alliance presentation of its two co-equal leaders, David Steel and David Owen; for the Labour exploitation of the health service run-down and for the Conservative counter-attacks over Labour's defence and taxation policies.

The polls, however, recorded little net change in party support during the campaign and the Conservatives, although losing 20 seats, mainly in the North, held on to their share of the national vote. The Labour party advanced only to 31 per cent, its second lowest vote in 60 years. The Alliance, down to

23 per cent of the vote, was only one seat worse off than in 1983.

The Conservatives did not suffer from the publicized rows within their campaign team: indeed, it was the only election in 30 years in which the party that was ahead did not fare worse than the polls had been predicting.

The 1987 election, despite its new professionalism, had less impact than any other in recent times. The government's inevitable return was the reward of the prosperity and social change that blunted the Labour party's attack and of the inability of the Alliance to repeat their upsurge of 1983. Mrs Thatcher became the first Prime Minister since Lord Liverpool in 1826 to win three successive elections.

1992

Mrs Thatcher's third term was her last. The economic recovery of the 1980s petered out in the years after the Stock Market crash of October 1987. The attempts to kept the pound in line with the Deutschmark had to be abandoned but when, in September 1990, Mrs Thatcher finally agreed to let Britain join the European exchange rate mechanism, it was at the unrealistic level of 2.95 Deutschmarks to the pound.

Meanwhile, the flagship policy of financing local government by a poll-tax instead of by property rates ran into deep trouble, and in 1990 provoked massive demonstrations. Mrs Thatcher's tenth anniversary in office in May 1989 marked the turn of the tide. Her ratings fell and her two most senior ministers, Nigel Lawson and Geoffrey Howe, resigned in protest at her high-handedness. In November 1990, when Michael Heseltine challenged her, she failed to win the required majority and reluctantly withdrew. John Major, her preferred successor, managed to beat Michael Heseltine and Douglas Hurd in the second round.

John Major's low-key approach did much to wipe clean the Conservative slate though the party continued to lose every by-election. The economy deteriorated further and the dissolution was put off until well into the fifth year of the parliament.

The Labour party under Neil Kinnock managed to set its house in order and to make itself ready to campaign professionally on a moderate pro-European programme. The Alliance had fallen apart over its attempts to merge the two parties into one after the 1987 election, and David Owen for a while led a new breakaway SDP. Paddy Ashdown took over the leadership of what came to be known as the Liberal Democratic party, which after a bad patch achieved three by-election victories. The Green party had a moment of glory when it won 15 per cent of the vote in the June 1989 elections to the European parliament, but its star quickly faded.

The 1992 campaign was protracted because the April 9 date had been long anticipated, so that in January and February both sides fought a preliminary battle, trying out their slogans and policies.

The Conservative manifesto, *The Best Future for Britain*, though 30,000 words long, contained few new themes. It proposed privatizing British Coal and parts of British Rail, and it promised to set up an Urban Regeneration Agency and a Millennium Fund.

Labour's manifesto, *It's Time to get Britain Working Again*,

Nicholas Garland, *Daily Telegraph*, 1 April 1992. © The Telegraph plc, London, 1992.

Table 2.14 General election of 9 April 1992

	Con	Lab	Lib D	Other	Total
Seats					
At dissolution	368	229	22	31	650
After election	336	271	20	24	651
Votes					
% of total	41.9	34.4	17.9	5.8	100.0
Change since 1987 (%)	−0.4	+3.6	−4.8	+1.5	
Conservative overall majority 21					
Turnout 77.7%					

MPs defeated: *Con* C. Patten, Mrs L. Chalker; *Lib D*: G. Howells; *SNP*: J. Sillars.
MPs retiring: *Con*: J. Amery, Sir I. Gilmour, Sir G. Howe, N. Lawson, J. Moore, C. Parkinson, N. Ridley, N. Tebbit, Mrs M. Thatcher, P. Walker, G. Younger; *Lab*: M. Foot, D. Healey, M. Rees; *Lib D*: Sir C. Smith; *SDP*: D. Owen.

endorsed the European Community and the Exchange Rate Mechanism. It promised a Scottish Parliament, a Bill of Rights and a Freedom of Information Act. It repudiated unilateralism and renationalization or any return to 1970s Trade Union legislation, but said that a Labour government would 'ensure that the market works properly' and would expand the economy.

The Liberal Democrats' *Changing Britain for Good* boasted of the party's realistic 'hairshirt policies' for economic reform, including a penny on income tax explicitly for educational improvements. It advocated far-reaching constitutional and economic changes.

The campaign was launched with the Budget on 10 March, which was countered by Labour's Shadow Budget on 16 March. Throughout the next three weeks the Conservatives, much aided by the tabloid press, harped on the theme that Labour would raise taxes, while Labour attacked the Conservative record and plans on employment and the Health Service.

The campaign was not exciting. Its most publicised feature

was 'The War of Jennifer's Ear', an irrelevant row concerning the ethics of a Labour broadcast about a little girl with a delayed ear operation. The opinion polls put Labour ahead – its lead peaked at 7 per cent on 1 April, the day of Labour's triumphal rally at Sheffield. On 9 April the pollsters were close to each other in suggesting a Labour lead of 1 per cent. But when the votes were counted that night, the Conservatives emerged 7.5 per cent ahead and with a clear majority of 21 seats, although nine ministers were defeated, including Chris Patten, the architect of the Conservative victory. It was unprecedented for a party to win four successive terms in office. It was also unprecedented for the opinion polls to go so far in misleading public expectations.

3 The Legal Framework

Elections are a matter both of form and of substance. There are legal rules – which are relatively permanent and, on the whole, faithfully obeyed – and there are customary practices which sometimes persist for a lifetime but which may be abruptly transformed or abandoned. The pages that follow are mainly concerned with the changes in the essential components of an election, the ways in which the contestants conduct themselves. But it is necessary to preface such a discussion with a record of the formal rules.

Elections take place under a strict framework of law which is generally taken for granted. Very little of it has changed since 1945. The rules about the conduct of constituency campaigns have seldom been the subject of dispute. They were largely devised in the latter part of the nineteenth century, notably in the *Ballot Act 1872* and the *Corrupt and Illegal Practices Prevention Act 1883*. These laws and their subsequent modifications were consolidated into the *Representation of the People Act 1949* and again into the *Representation of the People Act 1983*.

The *Ballot Act*, which regulates conduct at and around the polling booth, was designed to preserve the secrecy of the individual vote and by doing so to discourage bribery and intimidation in constituencies which sometimes contained less than a thousand electors. Its provisions are not wholly appropriate to modern needs: no one starting from scratch in 1988 would devise the current regulations for issuing and stamping ballot papers and for counting votes on a constituency basis rather than by wards or polling districts. But under these venerable rules the reputation of British elections for being fair and free from fraud has been preserved.

The *Corrupt Practices Act* contained provisions against treating and undue influence and other electoral abuses but it was important above all for its provision that 'no one other than the duly appointed agent' could incur expenses to promote a candidate's election. To this day, this has been the instrument for the effective restriction on spending at the constituency level. In fact, except in Northern Ireland, there have been no serious complaints since 1945 about malpractice by candidates, or their agents or supporters, and the number of prosecutions for personation or other misbehaviour at the polling stations has been negligible.

Elections are tightly regulated by law. Yet legal disputes have not been significant in any major way in post-war elections. A list of the Acts passed since 1945 in relation to elections is quite long, yet most of them have been quite uncontroversial.

Acts

House of Commons (Redistribution of Seats) Act 1947. This modified a 1944 Act to allow the Boundary Commissioners to recommend constituencies that deviated by more than 25 per cent from the national quota.

Representation of the People Act 1948. This abolished the business and university vote. It provided for postal voting. It abolished a qualifying period of residence for getting on the electoral register. It reduced the maximum for candidates' expenses. It limited the use of cars to take the electors to the poll. It enacted the comprehensive redistribution of seats proposed by the Boundary Commissioners.

House of Commons (Redistribution of Seats) Act 1949. This consolidated and amended the 1944 Act which provided for permanent Boundary Commissions and periodic redistribution of seats.

Representation of the People Act 1949. This consolidated the Representation of the People Act 1948 with a number of previous statutes, including the 1872 and 1883 Acts.

Electoral Registers Act 1949. This, as an economy, provided for the electoral register to be compiled once a year instead of once every six months as authorized in 1948.

Independent Television Act 1954. This barred any political advertising on commercial television.

Redistribution of Seats Act 1958. This extended the timetable for the routine redistribution of seats from '3 to 7 years' to '10 to 15 years'.

Representation of the People Act 1958. This abolished the 1948 limitation on the use of cars to take electors to the polls.

Representation of the People Act 1969. This lowered the age of voting to 18. It opened the door for party labels to appear on the ballot by allowing candidates six words of self-description. It also extended the hours of polling from 7 a.m. to 9 p.m. to 7 a.m. to 10 p.m.

Referendum Act 1975. This provided for the conduct and finding of the referendum on Britain's membership of the European Community.

European Assembly Elections Act 1978 (renamed in 1987 the *European Parliamentary Elections Act*). This made detailed provisions for direct elections to the European Parliament.

Representation of the People Act 1981. This made the nomination of a prisoner invalid and added two days to the duration of an election.

Representation of the People Act 1983. This consolidated the Representation of the People Act 1949 with various amendments since that time.

Representation of the People Act 1985. This raised the level of a deposit from £150 (where it had stood since its inception in 1918) to £500. It also gave the vote to British citizens abroad (for up to five years) and allowed holiday-makers to vote by post. It required local authorities to sell copies of the electoral register on computer tape.

Representation of the People Act 1989. This raised the permitted level of expenditure for by-election candidates to four times the general election amount. It also allowed Britons abroad to keep a vote for up to twenty years.

Boundary Commissions Act 1992. This required the Boundary Commissioners to report by the end of 1994 and thereafter every twelve years.

European Communities (Amendment) Act 1993. This implemented the Maastricht Treaty provisions entitling citizens of the European Union to vote in the country where they reside.

The way in which elections should be conducted was the subject of Speaker's Conferences in 1967 and 1973 but these produced no significant alterations. There was also a study by the Home Affairs Select Committee in 1983 which provided the basis for some of the reforms incorporated in the 1985 Act.

This book is concerned in the main with general elections. But it is worth remarking that the rules laid down for their conduct spill over to by-elections and to local elections, as well as to elections to the European Parliament. They also broadly governed the referendums which were initiated in the 1970s: these were in 1973 (and in 1983) in Northern Ireland over the maintenance of the Union; in 1975 in the UK as a whole over staying in Europe; and in 1979 in Scotland and in Wales over devolution.

Although electoral matters have seldom come before the Courts, it is worth listing the only significant cases since 1945.

Petitions

September 1955 Fermanagh and South Tyrone [1955] 105 LJ (successful – Unionist candidate replaces Sinn Fein MP because the election victor was a felon).

October 1955 Mid-Ulster (successful – Unionist candidate replaces Sinn Fein MP because the election victor was a felon. See *The Times*, 8 October 1955.).

April 1960 N. Kensington [1960] 2 All ER 150 (unsuccessful – technical points about actions of returning officer – action brought by Sir Oswald Mosley who won under 5 per cent of the vote).

July 1961 S.E. Bristol [1961] 3 All ER 354 (successful – Conservative candidate replaces T. Benn (Labour) because he was a peer).

December 1964 Kinross and South Perthshire [1965] SLR 186 (unsuccessful – party election broadcasts are not a chargeable expense).

November 1994 Devon West and Plymouth East (European Parliament Election) (unsuccessful – the returning officer did not err in accepting the nomination of a confusingly named candidate ['Literal Democrat']).

Boundaries

Harper and Others v. Home Secretary [1955] 1 All ER 331 (attempt to delay the redistribution of seats because of alleged errors by the Boundary Commission stopped by the Court of Appeal).

Foot and Others v. Boundary Commission [1983] QB 600 and 1 All ER 1099 (attempt to delay the redistribution of seats turned down by the High Court and the Court of Appeal).

Broadcasting and advertising

R. v. Tronoh Mines Ltd [1952] 1 All ER 697 (party advertising in the press at a general election does not break the law on expenses if it does not refer to a particular candidate).

Marshall v. BBC [1979] 2 All ER 80 (being shown in film in a programme is not 'taking part' – candidates can only take part in a programme if all candidates in the constituency consent).

Wilson v. Independent Broadcasting Authority [1979] SLR 279 (balance in a referendum is different from balance in a general election; but an attempt by the 'Labour Vote "No" Committee' to prevent all referendum broadcasts in Scotland on the ground that three of the four would be advocating a 'Yes' vote).

Wolfe v. Independent Broadcasting Authority (the Scottish National Party did not have the right to equal time in UK networked programmes. 1 April 1979. See Halsburys *Laws*, 4th edn, vol. 45, 574 (footnote 4) and 576 (footnote 12)).

Other Matters

[1951] AC 161 A clergyman of the Church of Ireland cannot be an MP (the Rev. J. G. Macmanaway, elected for Belfast West, was therefore unseated).

People no longer go to law about election results. This is partly because the law is expensive and slow; even if an election petition unseats the victor, much of the parliament will have elapsed. It is partly because the law is complex and double-edged – if one party has stepped over the line on expenditure in one constituency, it is likely that a rival party has transgressed elsewhere and mutual forbearance may obviate tit-for-tat litigation. But the main reason is that the law is broadly obeyed. There are no grounds to suppose that bribery, intimidation, personation or fraudulent registration (all well-attested nineteenth-century abuses) occur on any scale today. The reason may lie largely in general standards of civic virtue, but it also lies in the fact that systematic malpractice would be difficult to organize and the cost of being found out (in terms of damaged reputation rather than legal punishment) would be far greater than any marginal rewards in votes in a world where the outcome in 97 per cent of constituencies is decided by a majority of four figures or more.

4 Constituencies, Seats and Votes

Since 1918 at least it has been accepted that the country should be divided into roughly equal-sized constituencies so that each MP represents the same number of people. However, there was no change in boundaries from 1918 to 1945 despite huge movements of population. In 1935 the largest constituency, Romford, had 168,000 electors and by 1945 the smallest, North Southwark, had only 14,000. As an emergency measure 25 new seats were created in 1945 by subdividing the largest constituencies, and the House of Commons was increased from 615 members to 640 (see table 4.1). It was decided that, to avoid the recurrence of such anomalies, there should be a routine redistribution in the life of every parliament. The *Representation of the People Act 1948* provided for a 625 seat House and almost all constituencies were within 25 per cent of the national quotas.[1]

When the first routine redistribution was effected in 1955 (which raised the House to 630 members) 270 constituencies had their boundaries significantly altered. The process caused much unhappiness to MPs whose careers and local attachments were disrupted. As a result, the *Redistribution of Seats Act 1958* provided that the neutral Boundary Commissioners need only take action every 15 years.

In 1969 the Commissioners duly reported but, amid much controversy, the Labour government delayed implementing proposals that might have cost them a few seats, on the grounds that it was better to wait for the pending local government reform so that parliamentary and local government boundaries

Table 4.1 Number of House of Commons seats, 1945–1992

Year	England	Wales	Scotland	N. Ireland	Total
1945	510 (+7)	35 (+1)	71 (+3)	12 (+1)	628 (+12)
1950	506	36	71	12	625
1955	511	36	71	12	630
1974	516	36	71	12	635
1983	523	38	72	17	650
1992	524	38	72	17	651

Figures in parentheses are for 12 university seats which disappeared in 1950.

should coincide. When the Conservatives took office they immediately authorized the 1969 proposals (which in 1974 raised membership to 635). The next redistribution, because of legal complications, occupied the Boundary Commissioners from 1976 to 1983. There are now 651 constituencies. In 1983 all but 20 were within 20 per cent of their national quota. Scotland and Wales, however, are each over-represented compared with England (see table 4.2), because it has not been politically possible to reduce their number of MPs in line with their relative decline in population. If seats had been allocated on the basis of a national quota, Scotland would have 59 seats not 72, and Wales 32 seats not 38. Scotland and Wales are unhelpful territory for the Conservatives and their over-representation

Table 4.2 Electorate per seat, 1945–1992

Year	UK	England	Wales	Scotland	N. Ireland
1945*	52,494	52,206	51,330	46,940	70,505
1950	55,055	56,073	50,061	47,465	72,007
1955	55,330	56,350	50,028	47,718	72,833
1974	62,631	64,134	55,488	51,638	86,824
1983	64,913	67,194	55,628	53,985	61,778
1992	66,436	68,762	57,763	54,000	66,185

* The calculations for 1945 exclude the 12 university seats.

helps Labour. If electorates had been equal throughout the United Kingdom and the parties had retained the same ratio of seats within each component part, the Conservatives would have won 334 seats in 1992, not 336. In 1991 the Boundary Commissioners began a fresh review of constituencies with a view to reporting by 1994 or 1995. Anxiety about delays in the process which, once again, seemed certain to give seats to the Conservatives, led the Government to alter the law; the Boundary Commissioners were now required to produce a report by December 1994 and thereafter every twelve years and they were given extra resources to speed up their task.

That is not the only bias that boundary arrangements can produce. As the years go by, inner-city seats tend to become depopulated while suburban electorates grow. The 1955 boundaries, which in that year left 55,294 voters on average in Conservative constituencies and 55,508 in Labour constituencies, were still in force for the 1970 election, but by then Conservative seats had on average 67,638 electors and Labour ones 56,913.

There have been some sharp controversies and some unsuccessful law-suits about boundaries. In 1948 the Labour government was accused of gerrymandering when it unilaterally created 17 extra seats to redress the under-representation of urban areas; in the event, the seats divided evenly between the parties. In 1955 there were Labour protests and court actions against the anomalies inherent in using simultaneously a UK quota and English, Scottish and Welsh quotas. In 1969 the Conservatives were furious when Labour delayed the implementation of redistribution proposals that would hurt their interests. In 1982–3 Michael Foot and other leading Labour figures brought a protracted case against the Boundary Commissioners over the rules for allocating seats, particularly in London; the goal may have been to delay the redistribution until after the 1983 election – or just to delay the 1983 election.

However, despite these episodes, the constituency basis of British politics has been generally accepted. The Conservative and Labour parties have shown no inclination to change an electoral system which in alternation has given them full power. And the ordinary MP, it is plain, likes being a constituency

member, the sole parliamentary representative of and spokes-
man for a particular slice of Britain.

The single-member constituency system has major implications for British politics. It facilitates decisive election results,
enabling a party with a minority of votes to secure a clear
majority in parliament, and it discourages support for weaker
parties. Its properties used not to be fully appreciated. The
relationship between the votes cast for parties nationwide and
the division of seats in the House of Commons were once
regarded as a largely random matter. In 1909 J. Parker Smith
suggested to the Royal Commission on Electoral Systems that,
if votes divided nationwide in the ratio A:B, seats would divide
in the ratio $A^3:B^3$. But no one seems to have followed up this
'cube law' proposition. The *News Chronicle* in 1945 accom-
panied its accurate Gallup poll forecast of the percentage
division of the vote with the remark: 'It is impossible to base on
these results any forecast as to the probable distribution of
seats in the House of Commons ... The result of a British
general election under the present voting system [is unpredict-
able].'

It was only in 1947 that a more empirical attempt was made
to measure the relationship.[2] In 1949 I stumbled on the 'cube
law' and found that it worked with extraordinary accuracy for
the elections of 1931, 1935 and 1945; the findings were
published in *The Economist* on 7 January 1950. However, the
election of February 1950 belied the formula. It was not
because the system had lost the exaggerative quality implied in
the 'cube law' but because, following the redrawing of boundaries, Labour suffered through wasting votes in safe seats (42
out of the 50 largest majorities were in Labour constituencies);
Labour now needed almost 2 per cent more of the total vote to
win a general election than the Conservatives. However, over
subsequent years this safe seat bias against Labour largely
evaporated – or was cancelled by other biases, such as the
varying size of constituency electorates.

One central term used in the analysis of British elections is
'swing'. Swing is most commonly defined as the average of the
changes between one election and the next in the voting
percentages for the two main parties. Perhaps it is best

illustrated by two examples, one very simple, one slightly more complex.

	Year 1	*Year 2*	*Change*
Example A			
Con	60%	51%	−9%
Lab	40%	49%	+9%
			18% ÷ 2 = 9% Swing
Example B			
Con	38%	37%	−1%
Lab	36%	40%	+4%
Lib	26%	23%	
			5% ÷ 2 = 2.5% Swing

The virtue of the concept is that it reduces to a single statistic all the complex factors that lie behind any election result, cross-switches in party support as well as changes in electorate and in participation. Essentially swing indicates what has altered in the competitive position of the two parties. It is a massive simplification and, like all simplifications, it can at times produce paradoxes and distortions. But it has proved a very convenient tool for identifying those constituencies or regions which have diverged from the national pattern in a way that demands further investigation.

It has also been used successfully by election night commentators. 'The swing in Blanktown, the first constituency to complete its count, is 2.5 per cent. If the whole country were to behave like that, then the final outcome would be a Government majority of 40 seats', or 'The swing in the 20 seats that have reported so far averages 1.8 per cent; on that swing 40 seats should change hands'. The assumption of uniform swing underlying such forecasts has been found remarkably servicable.

In fact, the 'cube law' implied that, in an evenly balanced two-party situation, about 18 seats should change hands for every 1 per cent swing between the parties, making a difference of 36 to the parliamentary majority. From 1931 to 1970 this sort of exaggeration (under which a 1 per cent turnover in votes produces a 3 per cent turnover in seats) held good. But, even in such statistical matters, there are no iron laws of politics. Since

1970 the 'cube law' has ceased to apply. The exaggeration degenerated from a 'cube law' to a 'square law' (if votes are in the ratio A:B, seats will divide $A^2:B^2$) and then to an even lower proportion. If the 'cube law' had still been operating in 1983, Mrs Thatcher would have won 480 seats instead of 397; her clear majority over all parties would have been 310 not 146.

The reason for this change in the working of the system is that the number of marginal seats has declined sharply. This is due to demographic change, the movement of population and economic activity and not to boundary changes or any party manoeuvring. In 1955, 172 seats were held by Labour or Conservative with majorities of under 10 per cent; in 1987, the comparable figure was only 80. Rural seats have become far more Conservative. Urban centres have become far more Labour. In the 1955 election the Labour party elected MPs in a score of rural seats and were within striking distance in a number more; the Conservatives held a majority of the seats in Glasgow and Liverpool. In 1987 Labour held no rural seats in England and the Conservatives did not get even a quarter of the vote in any seat in Glasgow or Liverpool.[3]

In the 1950s a 1 per cent nationwide swing would have been enough to change a clear Conservative majority in the House of Commons into a clear Labour majority or vice versa. In the 1980s, because of the rise of centre and regional parties and the ending of Ulster Unionist support for the Conservatives, as well as the fall in the number of marginal seats, it would have taken a 4 per cent swing, as table 4.3 illustrates. The likelihood of a hung parliament has greatly increased as this no man's land between a clear victory for one side or the other has widened.

In 1992 the system worked in Labour's favour. They fared unexpectedly well in marginal seats. On a uniform movement from 1987, the 2.2 per cent swing that occurred would have returned 356 Conservatives and 251 Labour MPs; in fact, Labour won 20 more than that and the Conservatives 20 fewer. If the popular vote had tied at 38.1 per cent each, Labour would have won 320 seats to the Conservatives 282.

Because the existing arrangements have suited the interests of the two dominant parties, electoral reform has not been a major issue in British politics. The Liberals were converted to

Table 4.3 Difference in swing needed for clear majority in 1955 and 1992

	Con votes (%) (GB)	Lab votes (%) (GB)	Con seats	Lab seats	(Other seats)	Majority over second party	Majority over all parties
Actual result 1955	50.2	47.3	344	277	(9)	Con 67	Con 58
1.8% swing to Labour	48.4	49.1	316	305	(9)	Con 11	Con 2
2.5% swing to Labour	47.7	49.8	305	316	(9)	Lab 11	Lab 2

The difference between the swing that would leave Conservatives with a clear majority or Labour with a clear majority is 0.7%

	Con votes (%) (GB)	Lab votes (%) (GB)	Con seats	Lab seats	(Other seats)	Majority over second party	Majority over all parties
Actual result 1992	41.9	34.4	336	271	(44)	Con 65	Con 21
0.4% swing to Labour	41.5	34.8	326	279	(46)	Con 45	Con 2
3.8% swing to Labour	38.1	38.1	282	320	(49)	Lab 38	Lab −11
4.1% swing to Labour	37.8	38.5	276	326	(49)	Lab 52	Lab 2

The difference between the swing that would leave Conservatives with a clear majority or Labour with a clear majority is 3.7%

proportional representation in the 1920s only when they no longer had the muscle to force through the change which was necessary to their survival as a major party.

In the 1950s the anomalies of the electoral system were accepted tranquilly. Labour did not complain when it was defeated by the Conservatives in 1951 although it had 0.8 per cent more of the national vote. Conservative and Labour were each confident that the system would give them full power, turn and turnabout. At a time when they shared 95 per cent of the vote, there was perhaps nothing seriously objectionable about the harsh way that the system treated third parties. The large parties habitually justified the 'unfairness' of the system in pragmatic terms: 'It produces clear results'; 'we don't want coalition government'; or 'proportional representation would put the Liberals permanently in power'. They also pointed out that the two big parties had to be moderate as they wooed floating and minority votes.

In the 1970s, however, the electoral system became more controversial for two reasons. In the 1974 elections the Liberals won almost 20 per cent of the votes but only 2 per cent of the seats. This manifest injustice excited sympathy in some who had never had any particular interest in proportional representation. At the same time many Conservatives were appalled to see a Labour party that was committed 'to a fundamental and irreversible shift of power to working people' attaining a House of Commons majority on the basis of 39 per cent of the vote (or 29 per cent of the full electorate); as they looked for possible safeguards, such as a written constitution or a strengthened Upper House, several concluded that the best answer would lie in a reformed electoral system; proportional representation would mean that no party could get unfettered power unless it could secure almost 50 per cent of the vote. Opinion polls indicated majority support for proportional representation and, although neither the Conservatives nor the Labour front benches were converted, many influential Conservatives such as Lord Carrington, Jim Prior and Francis Pym endorsed the idea of reform. In 1976 a Hansard Society Commission under Lord Blake reported in favour of a version of the West German Additional Member System of proportional representation using single-member constituencies but then adding extra MPs to give the parties seats in proportion to their total vote. In 1983 an Alliance Commission, under Sir Henry Fisher, supported proportional representation using the single transferable vote in multi-member constituencies. Electoral reform was plainly on the national agenda in the event of a hung parliament. In 1993 a Labour Party Commission under Lord Plant recommended the adoption of 'the Supplementary Vote', an eccentric variant of the Alternative Vote. But, until a hung parliament occurs, the old system, passionately endorsed by Margaret Thatcher, is likely to survive, with its advocates pointing to the advantages of its decisive simplicity.

The simple majority single-member electoral system is hard on minor parties. Electors have every incentive to cast a *vote utile*, as the French say, and to mark a cross for the candidate with the best chance of defeating the candidate they most dislike. 'A Liberal vote is a wasted vote' was a common slogan during the party's lean years in the 1950s and 1960s.

As Liberal and Nationalist fortunes revived in the 1970s, people began to talk more exactly about tactical voting, about spontaneous or organized switching of votes. In by-elections opinion polls could give a cue. There is no doubt that some of the Alliance successes in the 1980s were due to Conservative or Labour voters switching to the Alliance once they saw that their candidate had less chance than the Alliance challenger of beating the traditional enemy. Labour voters helped Shirley Williams to her Crosby triumph in 1981 and Conservative switchers elected Rosie Barnes in Greenwich in 1987. In general elections the effects were smaller, but Curtice and Steed have shown that there was still a significant variation in swing depending on the tactical situation demonstrated by the previous election.[4] In 1987 it was certainly decisive in a few seats, while in many more it reinforced the lead of the second party over the third; over much of southern and rural England voters knew that the Alliance was the local alternative to the Conservatives and Labour was pushed to a poor third, while elsewhere Alliance support crumbled before Labour as the obvious challenger. In the light of this, it is difficult to take voting statistics as sincere statements of positive ideological or policy preference.

Notes

1 This measure also abolished the few remaining double-member seats, the last vestiges of the medieval arrangement under which all constituencies sent two members to parliament.
2 See the Appendix to R. B. McCallum and A. Readman, *The British General Election of 1945* (Oxford University Press, 1947).

3 For a full discussion of this see J. Curtice and M. Steed, 'Proportionality and exaggeration in the British electoral system', *Electoral Studies*, 1985.

4 See their Appendix to D. Butler and D. Kavanagh, *The British General Election of 1992* (Macmillan, 1992). See also J. Galbraith and N. Rae, 'A direct empirical test of the importance of tactical voting', *British Journal of Political Science*, 1989.

5 Franchise, Turnout and Voting Behaviour

In theory, every adult British, Irish or Commonwealth citizen resident in the United Kingdom has been entitled to vote throughout the period since 1945 (peers, lunatics and felons excepted). There have been only two major changes in the franchise. The *Representation of the People Act 1948* abolished the last vestiges of plural voting; graduates were no longer able to cast a second vote for one of the 12 university seats (which came to an end in 1950) and owners of business premises that lay in another constituency from their residence were no longer allowed to vote there as well. The *Representation of the People Act 1969* lowered the age of voting from 21 (or, in actual practice, from 21 years and six months) to just 18.

Other smaller changes have been made, especially by the *Representation of the People Act 1985* which allowed Britons residing overseas to stay on the register in their old constituency for up to 7 years, and the *Representation of the People Act 1989* extended this to 20 years. However in 1989 only 12,000 and in 1992 only 32,000 people took advantage of this provision, although millions were eligible.

However, legal eligibility does not make everyone able to vote. The electoral register cannot be perfect. It is compiled on the basis of place of residence on 10 October and, inevitably, there are duplications and gaps in this listing of 40 million names. Moreover, people move and people die while the register is in force.

The accuracy of the register has declined. A government study in 1951, comparing the electoral register with the more exhaustively compiled census, found that between 3 and 4 per cent of the eligible population were omitted and that an almost equal number of listed names referred to someone who was dead or who was properly on the register elsewhere. A second study in 1966 found a very similar error rate.

However, a third study after the 1981 census suggested that the error rate had doubled in both categories: almost 7 per cent of the names listed should not have been included and almost 7 per cent of qualified citizens were left out. The inaccuracies in the register had increased from one in thirty to one in fifteen. Not surprisingly, the error rate was much higher in city centres than in rural constituencies: an 18-year-old black youth in a deprived area had only a 50 per cent chance of being on the register, while a long-established inhabitant of a country town was over 99 per cent likely to be listed.

The accuracy of the register has major implications for the calculation of turnout. Public interest in elections would seem to have declined in terms of the most obvious measure: the percentage of the registered electorate who actually record a valid vote. Figure 5.1 shows the apparent decline in turnout from 84 per cent in 1950 to 75 per cent or less in recent elections. But well over a third of that decline has to be attributed to the lowered quality of the register. Moreover, the 1950 election was conducted not only on a uniquely accurate register but on one that had just come into force. An election which takes place in October is fought on a register that is 12 months from its compilation. In that period almost 2 per cent of

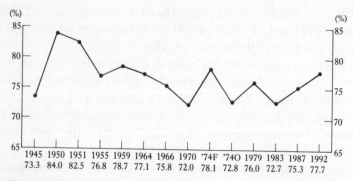

Figure 5.1 Turnout, 1945–1992.

the electorate will have died and a further 10–20 per cent will have moved; those who move can get a postal vote or they can return to their old locality to cast their ballot, but for many that is difficult or impracticable. It has been calculated that turnout is likely to be at least 0.5 per cent lower for every month that elapses after 15 February. The two elections in 1974 were fought on the same register; the decline in turnout from 78.1 per cent on 28 February to 72.8 per cent on 10 October may be attributed simply to factors such as these and not to any fall in popular interest. It is also worth pointing out that the mean turnout recorded between 1950 and 1992 (77.7 per cent) compares favourably with the figure of 73.6 per cent between 1922 and 1945.

The level of turnout from 1950 onwards was marginally increased by the 1948 introduction of postal voting for those finding it difficult to vote in person because they were ill, because they had moved house, because they lived too far from a polling station or because of the nature of their work. In 1985 the facility was extended to those who would be away on holiday. Securing the postal vote involves some minor form-filling and is a challenge to party organization. Its use varies widely even between similar constituencies. But in mainland Britain few constituencies have ever recorded as much as 5 per cent of their vote by post (Banff with 8.5 per cent in 1951 provides the record) and the average level has been barely 2 per cent of the total vote. The peak moments were in October 1951 (2.6 per cent) and October 1974 (3.0 per cent). The new opportunities for those on holiday was not much exploited in June 1987; the postal vote (2.4 per cent) only increased by 150,000 above the June 1983 figure (2.0 per cent). In 1992, in an April election, it fell to 2.1 per cent.

As the Conservatives have so much more professional an organization, and since they are strong among the form-filling classes, the postal vote has undoubtedly helped them to a few extra victories in each election. Cautious estimates suggest that they owed ten or so seats to the postal vote in most elections from 1950 to 1970 but, with the falling number of marginal seats, the figure in recent contests has been only four or five. But this impact of the postal vote was sufficient to reduce

Labour from a viable to a hairsbreadth majority in three close elections (1950, 1964 and October 1974) and to give the Conservatives their clear majority in one (1951).

It is significant that in the marginal Northern Irish constituencies, where political zeal is intense, the postal vote has been much larger. The all-time record for the percentage cast in one constituency was supplied by Fermanagh and South Tyrone with 14.4 per cent in October 1974.

There are other measures of popular involvement in elections. According to the Gallup poll, the percentage of the electorate claiming to have gone to an election meeting fell from 30 per cent in 1951 to 1 per cent in 1992. The number claiming to have canvassed for their party fell from 4 per cent in 1951 to 2 per cent in 1987. But television, a negligible factor in 1951, has come into its own. In 1992, 80 per cent of the electorate watched a party election broadcast and 90 per cent watched at least some television newscasts.

The number of electors grew from 33 million in 1945 to 43 million in 1992. Most of this increase was the result of the natural growth of population but the 1969 lowering of the voting age to 18 added almost three million to the total eligible for inclusion on the register.

The change in the electorate, however, is far greater than the mere increase in numbers implies. Four-fifths of those on the 1945 register were dead by 1992. Half of those on the 1992 register could not have cast their first ballot before 1970; a quarter could never have voted in an election that did not return Mrs Thatcher to Downing Street. Even in a short period deaths and comings of age can make a difference. If the 1964 election had been decided by those on the register in 1959 Harold Wilson would not have won.

Obviously, the life experience and the exposure to politics of someone born in 1960 is very different from that of someone born in 1900. The world changed greatly between 1945 and 1992, and Britain's place in it was transformed. In 1945 the United Kingdom was still a world power; the red on the map covered a quarter of the inhabited land mass and British real income per head was only topped by the United States and Canada. By 1992, Britain could be caricatured as merely an

important offshore island of Europe, without significant overseas possessions and twentieth in the world league in terms of
per capita wealth. Compared to such a revolution, the changes
in Britain's party battle in and the style and administration of
her elections look trivial. But it is worth stressing some of the
social changes that have overtaken society over a forty-year
period. The categories in table 5.1 are somewhat arbitrary and
the statistics are not all exactly comparable. But they do show
the very different Britain that has developed over the past forty
years. People are, on average, twice as rich and more than twice
as likely to own their own homes; they have acquired cars and
telephones; and they have had more education. Non-manual

Table 5.1 Social and political change, 1950–1992

No. on electoral register	34m	(1950)	43m	(1992)
Gross Domestic Product per head (in constant terms)	100	(1951)	224	(1992)
Value of 1951 (£)	£1	(1951)	7p	(1992)
Owner-occupied homes (%)	29	(1951)	67	(1991)
Adults owning shares (%)	7	(1958)	22	(1991)
Households with television (%)	10	(1950)	98	(1991)
Car in household (%)	12	(1950)	65	(1990)
Telephone in household (%)	12	(1950)	87	(1990)
Still at school over 14 (%)	38	(1938)	100	(1992)
17–19 age group entering full-time higher education (%)	6	(1950)	22	(1992)
Population over 65 (%)	10	(1950)	18	(1990)
One-person households (%)	11	(1951)	26	(1991)
Of New Commonwealth origin (%)	0.5	(1950)	5	(1992)
Employed in manual jobs (%)	64	(1951)	45	(1991)
Working population in manufacturing and mining (%)	39	(1951)	19	(1990)
Unemployed (%)	1.5	(1951)	10	(1992)
Voting Labour (%)	49	(1951)	34	(1992)
Voting Conservative (%)	48	(1951)	42	(1992)
Voting for other parties (%)	3	(1951)	24	(1992)

workers now outnumber manual workers. It is true that by 1987 there were far more one-person households, far more old people, far more citizens from the New Commonwealth, and far more unemployed, but the most central feature of the changed electorate was, however, that it had moved sharply towards the middle class in occupation and consumption patterns – and away from Labour in voting patterns.

The reasons why people vote as they do and why they change their allegiance are still obscure, despite an ever-growing body of academic and commercial research since the 1950s.[1] It is plain that for a majority of people partisanship is a habit of mind, a loyalty that continues, election after election. Most citizens vote as they always voted – and usually as their parents voted before them. In successive pairs of elections since 1945 the average nationwide swing between Conservative and Labour has been only 2.8 per cent. The highest was 5.2 per cent between October 1974 and May 1979 and the lowest 0.9 per cent between February 1950 and October 1951. The actual number of switches has, of course, been considerably greater than this since people move in both directions in a cancelling way, as well as to third parties. However, the great bulk of voters does not change parties. Explanations of electoral behaviour often focus on the few who change rather than the many who do not.

Partisanship has been closely correlated with class and with region. Labour, from the start, drew especial support in areas with a high proportion of manual workers, particularly in areas of heavy industry. But it has also been disproportionately strong in Wales while, in recent years, Scotland and parts of the north of England, too, have become even more Labour than their class basis would suggest. At the same time, the Conservatives have achieved a virtual monopoly of representation in suburban and rural England. Labour, which won a majority of the seats in East Anglia in 1945, won only one (in Norwich) in 1987; Oxford East and Bristol South were the only other southern constituencies outside London that returned a Labour MP in 1987. Table 5.2 shows the transformation in British electoral geography.

Obviously, one explanation lies in the relative prosperity of

Table 5.2 Long-term geographic changes in party support and in representation, 1955–1992

Region	Two-party swing to Con 1955–87 (%)	Con seats in region (%)		
		1955	1992	Change
South	+8.9	72	80	+8
Midlands	+5.9	41	61	+20
North	−8.6	45	33	−16
Wales	+0.6	17	16	−1
Scotland	−19.1	51	15	−36
Great Britain	+7.4	54	53	−1

In 1955, 45 per cent of Labour MPs came from the Midlands and the South; in 1992 only 32 per cent did.
Source: J. Curtice and M. Steed, Appendix to D. Butler and D. Kavanagh, *The British General Election of 1992* (Macmillan, 1992).

the south, enhanced by Britain's increasing involvement with Europe and with world markets. It is far easier for voters in deprived Liverpool to identify with Labour than for their fellow citizens in prosperous Essex.

The north/south dichotomy must not be pressed too far. In 1992 the Conservatives still held 53 out of the 160 seats that lie between Cheshire and the Scottish border; it is only in Scotland, where they fell from 36 seats in 1955 to 11 in 1992, that their situation has deteriorated so spectacularly (though Liverpool and Manchester where the Conservatives had half the MPs in 1955 and now have none should also be mentioned).

Class is still linked in a major way with partisanship but the link has declined, as table 5.3 shows. The percentage voting with their 'natural' class party has fallen from almost two-thirds to under one-half.

These figures can be deceptive and there is considerable academic argument about the extent of the decline. Definitions of class cannot be constant and, even where the categories change little over the years, the proportion of the population

Table 5.3 Class and voting behaviour, 1945–1992

| | 1945 | | 1955 | | 1964 | | Oct 1974 | | 1983 | | 1987 | | 1992 | |
	Non-manual	Manual	Non-manual	Manual	Non-manual	Manual	Non-manual	Manual	Non-manual	Manual	Non-manual	Manual	Non-manual	Manual
Con (%)	63	29	70	32	62	28	51	24	55	35	54	35	55	32
Lab (%)	28	62	23	62	22	64	25	57	17	42	18	43	22	52
Lib/Alln (%)	9	9	6	6	16	8	24	20	28	22	28	22	23	16
Non-manual Conservatives plus manual Labour as % of all voters	62		65		63		54		47		48		54	

Source: A. Heath, R. Jowell and J. Curtice, *How Britain Votes* (Pergamon, 1985).

falling within each category changes. As table 5.1 shows, manual employees fell from 64 per cent to 45 per cent of the workforce between 1951 and 1990. But even among manual workers the percentage voting Labour went down from about two-thirds in the 1950s and 1960s to under one-half in the 1980s. Table 5.4 shows the social structure of voting at the end of the period, using the conventional ABC market research classifications. Table 5.5, using Anthony Heath's definitions, gives a slightly different picture.

Other cleavages – sex and age (important in some other countries) – have mattered little in British politics, although the addition of 18–21-year-olds to the register in 1969 probably cut Mr Heath's majority from 60 to 30 in 1970 and made the decisive difference in the two 1974 elections. Except in Northern Ireland, religion has played almost no overt part in British politics since the war. But 80 years ago it was as important as class in determining party support. Since many people vote as their parents did – and indeed as their grandparents and great grandparents did – traces of that old religious divide are still to be found in the continuing association between nonconformity and support for the Liberal and Labour parties as against the Anglican leaning towards Conservatism.

Immigration and its control provided a key question in British politics in the 1960s. Yet no major party took up an overtly racist stand and no party undid the other's restrictive immigration laws. The race question never became an explicit election issue on a nationwide scale (though, as in Smethwick in 1964, it was occasionally exploited at constituency level). Even Enoch Powell's speech envisaging 'the Tiber flowing with much blood' which evoked such extraordinary public reaction in April 1968 was not translated into electoral action. Yet there is no doubt that race has had a major impact on voting figures over the past 20 years. About 5 per cent of the electorate are of New Commonwealth origin and their rate of turnout is now similar in proportion to the national average. But, for reasons both of class and race, four out of five of their votes have gone to the Labour party, adding between 1 and 2 per cent to Labour's share of the national vote: however, because the black population is so heavily concentrated in safe Labour

Table 5.4 How Britain voted in 1992 (market research categories)

	Class			Trade union member	Sex		Age (year)				All
	ABC1	C2	DE		Men	Women	18–24	25–34	35–54	55+	
All	43	27	30	23	49	51	14	19	33	34	100
Con	54	39	31	31	41	44	35	40	43	46	43
Lab	22	40	49	46	37	34	39	38	34	34	35
Alln	21	17	19	19	18	18	19	18	19	17	18

Source: MORI.

Table 5.5 How Britain voted in 1987 (British Election Study categories)

	Con	*Lab*	*Other*	*N*
Salariat (%)	52.9	16.4	30.7	(782)
Routine non-manual (%)	51.5	24.0	24.4	(753)
Petty bourgeoisie (%)	63.6	16.8	19.5	(220)
Foremen (%)	38.6	34.5	26.9	(171)
Working class (%)	30.6	47.4	22.0	(1134)

These percentages are for individuals classified according to their *own* occupations.

seats, it has not made a proportionate difference to Labour strength in parliament.

In all classes the most striking change in behaviour came in the 1960s. Voters became much more volatile. The early post-war years had shown unprecedented electoral stability. For instance, between 1945 and 1965 only 8 per cent of by-elections led to a change in party control; between 1966 and 1992, however, the figure was 30 per cent. Since 1945 the average fluctuation between the highest and lowest reading for Conservative support within each calendar year, as measured by Gallup's monthly readings, went up decade by decade table 5.6 shows. Pollsters have found people becoming less and less strongly attached to their party.

Table 5.6 Fluctuations in voting support for the Conservatives within each year, 1945–1992

1945–54	5.5%
1955–64	7.5%
1965–74	9.2%
1975–84	12.5%
1985–92	20.6%

The reasons for this increase in volatility are manifold. First, the electorate has been exposed to more education. In 1945, 95 per cent of voters had left school at 14. Now all children must remain until their sixteenth birthday and many more than before stay on for university or further education. A more sophisticated electorate is more likely to break away from voting out of habit or inherited loyalty.

Secondly, social conditions have produced cross-pressures on many people. The solid working-class basis of Labour support is often eroded as members of families move into white-collar jobs and as the ownership of houses and cars spreads. The Labour party's natural constituency became increasingly threatened as house ownership grew from 29 per cent in 1951 to 67 per cent in 1992 and as the proportion of individuals in non-manual occupations rose from 36 per cent to 51 per cent of the workforce.

A third cause of volatility must lie in the experience of alternating governments in the 1960s and 1970s. The country was conscious of the decline in its world status, and of its slippage in the international prosperity league. But as Labour and Conservative governments took over from each other and demonstrated that the remedies advocated in opposition did nothing to set things to rights, it became far harder to remain a true believer in the virtue and skill of any one party or, conversely, to blame one special set of politicians for the country's ills.

Fourthly, the rise of third parties as credible forces, the Nationalists in Scotland and Wales, and the Liberals and then the Social Democrats in Britain as a whole, made it easier to desert the old parties without going all the way over to the hated enemy – and once voters had been unfaithful to their traditional party it became easier for them to be unfaithful again.

The most important cause of increased volatility was, however, the abrupt arrival around 1959 of television as the main source of political communication; this transformed the way in which parties and the political struggle were perceived (see pp. 106–7).

It is tempting to seek patterns in voting, regularities that represent laws of social science. But there are no eternal patterns. The 'cube law', for many years an accurate measure of the exaggeration in the relation between seats and votes inherent in Britain's majoritarian electoral system, ceased to apply in the 1970s. Equally, some theories about the determinants of voting can go astray. The 'deferential Conservative', the working man choosing to be governed by his betters, detected by R. T. McKenzie in the 1950s and discussed in *Angels in Marble*, has not loomed large in recent literature. Or, to take another example, *Political Change in Britain*, written in the 1960s, pointed out that, as most people voted as their parents did and as Labour did not come into equal contention with the Conservatives until 1945, there was an age bias in the electorate; more Conservatives than Labour voters were dying and more Labour than Conservative voters were entering the electorate, and therefore, up to the 1990s, other things being equal, there would be a swing of something like a quarter of one per cent per annum from Conservative to Labour, simply due to differential mortality. The theory, the logic and the evidence behind this argument may have been impeccable but other things were not equal; increasing volatility and changing social patterns more than cancelled any advantage that Labour was receiving from the age structure of the electorate.

A different type of explanation of voting behaviour was put forward very convincingly in 1970. Goodhart and Bhansali showed a remarkable correlation between unemployment figures and the ups and downs in the monthly Gallup poll. From 1946 to 1968 it seemed that one more person unemployed meant 26 votes lost to the party in power eight months later. But, at the very moment that this statistical regularity was being propounded, it ceased to be valid. Indeed, if the Goodhart/Bhansali formula had been valid in 1983, Mrs Thatcher would actually have had no votes at all.[2]

To point to the failure of these attempts to explain voting is not to deride them or the many other theories that have been explored in the recent academic literature. The effort to find broad forces behind the mass movements of voting support will go on challenging students and political operators. There is no doubt that it has fed back into the changing pattern of electioneering over the past 40 years.

Notes

1 See Ivor Crewe, *British Electoral Behaviour 1945–1987* (Blackwell, 1989).
2 C. Goodhart and R. Bhansali, 'Political economy', *Political Studies*, 1970.

6 The Timing of Elections and the Party Battle

Every parliament has to be dissolved five years from the date of its first meeting (unless extended by special legislation, as it was from 1940 to 1945). But of the 12 complete parliaments since the war only one (1959–64) has run its full course (table 6.1). Three parliaments were dissolved after 19 months at most because of small or non-existent majorities, but all the rest lasted over three and a half years. Elections are unpopular and the result can never be guaranteed; Prime Ministers have been reluctant to go to the country without a very good excuse until the parliament has reached its last year. In April 1955 Sir Anthony Eden wanted a personal mandate when he took over from Sir Winston Churchill when the parliament was three and a half years old. In February 1974 Edward Heath was, after three and a half years, forced by the miners into an appeal to the country. Margaret Thatcher sought re-election after just four years in May 1983 and again in May 1987; she liked a summer election and was assured each time that her prospects were excellent. Harold Wilson did the same in May 1970 when Labour unexpectedly surged up in the polls. But in none of these cases – especially 1970 – could the opposition complain, since they had long been challenging the government to go to the country.

But, of course, the freedom to decide on the election date is a major advantage to the incumbent government. They can time the dissolution to coincide with an upsurge in the economy – or to get it over with before prosperity declines. They can even stimulate the economy to make the climate right for their

Table 6.1 Election timetables, 1945–1992

Year	Duration of previous parliament (years/days)	Date of election announcement	Date of dissolution	Date of poll	From announcement to poll (days)
1945	9/172	23 May	15 June	5 July	43
1950	4/138	11 Jan	3 Feb	23 Feb	43
1951	1/217	19 Sep	5 Oct	25 Oct	36
1955	3/187	15 Apr	6 May	26 May	41
1959	4/103	8 Sep	18 Sep	8 Oct	30
1964	4/341	15 Sep	25 Sep	15 Oct	30
1966	1/166	28 Feb	10 Mar	31 Mar	31
1970	4/41	18 May	29 May	18 June	31
1974F	3/225	7 Feb	8 Feb	28 Feb	21
1974O	0/198	18 Sep	20 Sep	10 Oct	22
1979	3/171	29 Mar	7 Apr	3 May	35
1983	4/4	9 May	13 May	9 June	31
1987	3/334	11 May	15 May	11 June	31
1992	4/274	11 Mar	13 Mar	9 Apr	30

purposes. In 1955 and 1970 there were strong allegations about give-away budgets; the accusation was also made in 1966 and 1987. And in 1964 and again in 1978 the election was un-expectedly postponed for six months because the Prime Minister of the day hoped for improved conditions.

It cannot be said, however, that any post-war election has been a snap affair designed to catch the opposition unprepared. Governments have, of course, called elections at the time that best suited them, but the impending dissolution has always been well canvassed. After a parliament has passed the halfway mark, the timing of the next election becomes standard material for every political columnist in search of a theme, as well as providing the subject of continuous gossip at Westminster. There have always been complaints about the party in power manipulating the economy to produce the right electoral climate but there have never been serious objections to the actual calling of the election or to the duration of the contest.

Whether it is desirable for Prime Ministers to have such power over the choice of election date has not been much argued. Britain, like most other parliamentary democracies, has never seriously contemplated fixed-term parliaments. Governments like control over dissolution not only for the tactical timing of elections but as an instrument of discipline. If government MPs know that a defeat on a major issue will lead the Prime Minister to dissolve parliament, they have a powerful incentive to ensure they vote loyally on key occasions.

Election campaigns have always lasted three weeks or so. From 1918 to 1982, 20 days had to elapse between the dissolution of parliament and the poll (ten days from the issue of the writs to the close of nominations and ten days from then to polling day). Because of the troubles in Northern Ireland and the need to allow extra time to check if any felons had been nominated, the 20 days rule was extended in 1982 to 23 days (or longer if any Bank Holidays intervened).

However, elections are seldom confined to the statutory minimum period. It is true that in 1974 the announcement of the 28 February election was made on 7 February, only the day before the dissolution of parliament. But usually between ten and 20 days' additional notice has been given.

British elections are brief – but not too brief. Nationally, and at the constituency level, politicians have expressed doubts about their ability to sustain interest in a campaign that lasts even as much as 20 days. Some weeks are needed to prepare election addresses and to complete a full canvass, but the high-pressure intrusion of politics into everyday life for even 20 days is seen by many as counter-productive. The broadcasting authorities need the time to fit in 15 or so party election broadcasts on weekdays and to allow their weekly flagship programmes to give one slot each to three major groupings. But the parties themselves have become increasingly reluctant to launch their manifestos until after the dissolution, and the Conservatives especially have shown themselves skilled in holding back their public efforts for a crescendo in the final week. By American standards, British campaigns are extraordinarily short and intense. But it was an American who described the quiet beginnings of a British election as the lull before the lull. For politicians and the media, elections are a very busy time; for most citizens their main consequence is a short-term disruption of their television fare.

British elections are still nominally about choosing individuals to represent 600–plus constituencies in the House of Commons, as they have been for seven centuries. But in fact British elections are a choice between parties, between rival teams seeking to provide the government of the country for the next few years. Party labels only appeared on the ballot paper in 1970, but throughout this century there is no doubt that the overwhelming majority of votes has been cast for national party reasons and not because of the merits of the individual candidates.

The number of candidates has fluctuated over the 13 post-war elections from 1,376 in 1951 to 2,948 in 1992; in other words, the average number of candidates in each constituency has varied between 2.2 and 4.5. The Conservative and Labour parties have contested virtually every seat on every occasion. In 1951 – the extreme case – voters faced a simple choice: there was a straight fight between Conservative and Labour in 485 out of 613 seats in Great Britain. The Liberals, though fighting more seats in the 1960s, only moved to a full slate in 1974, and the Scottish and Welsh Nationalists in 1970. Independents and minor parties peaked at 930 candidates in 1992; in 1987 the increase in the deposit (from £150 to £500) reduced their number to 318 but the fall was short-lived. Since 1945 less than 1 per cent of votes has gone to independent candidates, and since 1950 only four members (all dissident sitting MPs) have been elected in mainland Britain without the support of a major party;[1] in 1987 not one of the 240 mainland candidates who were not Conservative, Labour, Alliance or Nationalist secured as much as 4 per cent of the vote.

For most of the period the Conservative and Labour parties completely dominated the scene. But in the past 20 years, the two-party dominance in votes has fallen sharply (table 6.2). In seats the change has been less, but the House of Commons, which contained only seven MPs from outside the two main

Table 6.2 Two-party dominance, 1950–1992

Year	Con and Lab combined		Third and minor parties	
	% of total vote	*% of total seats*	*% of total vote*	*% of total seats*
1950	89.6	98.3	10.4	1.7
1951	96.8	98.6	3.2	1.4
1955	96.1	98.6	3.9	1.4
1959	93.2	98.9	6.8	1.1
1964	87.5	98.6	12.5	1.4
1966	88.8	97.8	11.2	2.2
1970	89.4	98.1	10.6	1.9
1974F	74.9	94.2	25.1	5.8
1974O	75.0	93.9	25.0	6.1
1979	80.9	95.6	19.1	4.4
1983	70.0	93.0	30.0	7.6
1987	73.1	91.8	26.9	8.2
1992	76.3	93.2	23.7	6.7

parties in 1959, had 44 such MPs in 1992. The party battle has been transformed by the rise of the centre; the Liberals, later reinforced by the Social Democrats, increased their representation from a minimum of five (in 1957) to a maximum of 27 (in March 1987). The scene has also been changed by events in Northern Ireland and by the arrival of Welsh and Scottish Nationalists.

From 1922 to 1966 nine of the 12 Northern Ireland seats were firmly in the hands of the Ulster Unionists and they sometimes secured the other three. In 1959 and 1964 all 12 seats returned Unionist MPs – and, in those days, the Unionists in almost all circumstances conformed to the Conservative whip. After the troubles broke out in Ulster in 1968, it became increasingly difficult for any Northern Ireland politician to side wholeheartedly with any mainland party; since 1974 none has done so. In 1983 Northern Ireland representation was increased to 17, and in 1987 the Ulster MPs included 13

Unionists of various shades and four from the Catholic community.

Plaid Cymru elected its first member in a 1966 by-election and the Scottish Nationalists their first (since 1945) in a 1967 by-election. Since then, these two parties have contested almost every seat in Wales and Scotland. Plaid Cymru has little hope outside the five predominantly Welsh-speaking constituencies but since 1974 it has always held between two and four of these. The SNP challenge is more widespread. Fourteen of Scotland's 72 seats have at some time seen an SNP victory, but only in the 1974 elections did the party return more than three MPs. None the less, the existence of a full slate of nationalist candidates in Scotland and Wales has changed the nature of elections in those countries, just as the universal presence of a Liberal or Alliance candidate, often as the most serious challenger to the incumbent MP, has changed electioneering from the simple Conservative versus Labour model of the 1950s. Conservative and Labour provided the top two candidates in 599 (96 per cent) seats in 1955 but in only 283 (44 per cent) in 1983. Both on the national electoral scene and in the House of Commons the prime battle has continued to be between Conservative and Labour, but in the 1980s a majority of electors and a majority of MPs had a different sort of fight in their own constituency.

Note

1 These were Sir D. Robertson (1959, ex-Con, Caithness and Sutherland); S. O. Davies (1970, ex-Lab, Merthyr); D. Taverne (1972 and 1974, ex-Lab, Lincoln); E. Milne (1974, ex-Lab, Blyth).

7 Changing MPs

Parties maintain a great continuity. In every general election since 1950 nine seats out of ten have stayed with the same side. Few MPs change parties and MPs serve on average for about 15 years: some endure for 40. In 1993 the House of Commons contained Edward Heath and Tony Benn, first elected in 1950. John Major became Prime Minister 11 years after his first election, but that was quite exceptional. Harold Wilson became Prime Minister 19 years after his first election; Edward Heath and Margaret Thatcher each took 20 years to get to the top and Clement Attlee 23. The other five post-war Prime Ministers went to No. 10 Downing Street more than 30 years after entering parliament.

But the long service of members and ministers does not mean that parties stay the same. A politician and his policies change with circumstances and with the surrounding people. The composition of the parliamentary parties is not what it was in 1945. By broad measures of social background the alteration has not been great as table 7.1 shows. The Conservatives continue to be a party of public school and university-educated professionals and businessmen, though rather less Etonian and aristocratic than years ago. Labour has changed more, with a decline in manual workers and an increase in graduates. Miners who made up 15 per cent of the parliamentary Labour party in 1951, were down to 4 per cent in 1992. Women, though still a 9 per cent minority, are better represented in both parties. 1987 saw the election of the first black MPs for 50 years and in 1992 six were elected. The Liberals and Social

Table 7.1 Background of MPs in 1951 and 1992

	Conservative MPs		Labour MPs	
	1951	*1992*	*1951*	*1992*
Professional	41%	39%	35%	42%
Business	37%	38%	9%	8%
Miscellaneous	22%	22%	19%	28%
Manual worker	–	1%	37%	22%
Public school	75%	62%	23%	14%
Etonians	25%	10%	1%	1%
University	65%	73%	41%	61%
Oxbridge	52%	45%	19%	16%
Median age	47	48	52	49
Women	1%	6%	2%	14%

Democrats and the Nationalists have been almost uniformly middle class in occupational background.

But much more has changed than this suggests. Membership of the House of Commons is now nearer to a full-time job. Senior trade-union officials, like major industrialists, no longer find it practicable to serve as MPs. The Conservatives have more self-made businessmen than 40 years ago and fewer 'knights of the shire'; the Labour party has more MPs from teaching and local government backgrounds. Furthermore, MPs spend their time differently. They now all have their own offices and telephones around the Palace of Westminster with a secretary and sometimes a research assistant. They have far more constituency cases to take up with departments and they are the object of far more attention from pressure groups. There is more committee work in both standing and select committees, as well as in party and inter-party consultative bodies.

Candidates are still chosen by constituency parties. For Conservative and Labour a committee – on average about 50 strong – chooses from a short list. Although the national parties have to endorse the choice, they have shown themselves signally unable to determine it or to parachute in the candidate they would like. The qualities sought by constituency parties have changed subtly. In the 1950s the identikit Tory was a public school, Oxbridge man in his thirties, with a good war record and a solid base in party activity. Labour was already moving from the stalwart trade unionist to the manager or teacher; the reduction in Labour MPs in the 1980s, with the party driven back to its working-class northern heartlands, has in fact slightly restored the trade-union share of representation.

MPs once elected have almost always been renominated by their local party if they wanted to be. Some MPs may have retired before they intended because it was clear that achieving reselection might present difficulties. But the number of cases where an MP has been explicitly rejected by the constituency party is very small. Over the ten general elections from 1950 to 1979 only 17 Conservative MPs and 16 Labour MPs seem to have fallen into this category; in other words, during the average parliament, deselection ended less than 0.5 per cent of MPs' careers. In 1983, however, at least six Conservative and 12 Labour MPs had to give up their parliamentary career because the redistribution of seats left them without a constituency. Before the 1983 and 1987 elections a few Labour MPs were sacked under the new provisions for reselection introduced in 1981. There were eight such casualties in 1983, six in 1987 and three in 1992; but these figures represented less than 2 per cent of sitting Labour MPs. On the other hand, fear of deselection looms slightly larger in members' minds than it used to, and sometimes causes them to modify their behaviour.

Overall, however, the ordinarily conscientious member in all parties remains, as always, fairly sure of renomination. Moreover, if a member of any distinction is defeated by the voters, he can usually find another home. The absence of a locality rule enables MPs to carpet-bag around the country. In the post-war period Harold Macmillan, Michael Foot, Alec Douglas-Home, Geoffrey Howe and Tony Benn are among the many who have moved to represent constituencies far distant from their original seat. But such mobility does not alter the enduring importance of the link between member and constituency. It may not make much difference to the ordinary elector who represents them (barely 50 per cent can name their MP and less than 20 per cent can offer any detailed information about him or her), yet MPs are enormously aware of their status as ambassadors for their constituency. Their ever-growing mailbags have if anything increased their overwhelming sense of political and personal identity as 'the member for . . .'.

The electoral advantages of being an incumbent MP are not great, but they do seem to have increased. In the 1950s it was impossible to detect a significant difference between the swings in seats where a sitting MP was fighting again and those where a newcomer was standing. In the 1960s Philip Williams detected a slight bonus for MPs at the end of their first or second term – and a deficit for some veterans who perhaps had outstayed their welcome.[1] More recently, John Curtice and Michael Steed have found that MPs who had gained a seat in one election secured 1,000 more votes in the next than would have been expected on a uniform swing.[2] Members who have just won marginal seats have every incentive to be energetic and the secretarial and other facilities now available give them increased opportunity to build up support through direct mail, local radio and well-publicized devotion to constituency cases.

Notes

1 P. M. Williams, 'Two notes on the British electoral system', *Parliamentary Affairs*, Winter 1966–7, pp. 13–30.
2 See their Appendix to D. Butler and D. Kavanagh, *The British General Election of 1992* (Macmillan, 1992), pp. 340–1.

8 The Cost of Elections

Elections cost money. But by world standards British campaigns have been relatively economical. Although the amount spent on campaigning at the national level has greatly increased in recent years, constituency expenditure has remained modest. There has never been any requirement for party headquarters to publish detailed accounts of what they spend on campaigns. However, in his authoritative *British Political Finance 1830–1980*, and in subsequent writings, Michael Pinto-Duschinsky has arrived at the figures for central expenditure during general elections given in table 8.1. The 1987 figures for these central expenses, which are not regulated by law, contrast sharply with the total spent by all the candidates in all the constituencies, duly constrained by legal limits. For the Conservatives the £9.0m spent centrally has to be set against £2.8m spent locally; for Labour the figures are £4.2m and £2.5m. The Alliance spent £1.9m centrally and £1.6m locally in 1983, and £1.8m centrally and £2.2m locally in 1987. (A limited portion of all this central expenditure went in grants to the constituencies so there is some double counting.)

Elections at the constituency level are, indeed, inexpensive compared to most democracies. Allowing for inflation, the amount spent by each candidate is far lower now than in the 1950s, let alone in 1900 as table 8.2 shows. Since the electorate increased by a third between 1945 and 1987, the amount spent per elector fell even more. No money can be spent to further a candidature except by the authorized agent of the candidate. In

Table 8.1 Central election expenditure by parties, 1945–1992

Year	Conservative (£)	Labour (£)
1945	50–100,000	51,000
1950	135,000	84,000
1951	112,000	80,000
1955	142,000	73,000
1959	631,000	239,000
1964	1,233,000	538,000
1966	350,000	196,000
1970	630,000	526,000
1974F	680,000	440,000
1974O	950,000	524,000
1979	2,333,000	1,566,000
1983	3,800,000	2,258,000
1987	9,000,000	4,200,000
1992	11,196,000	10,597,000

Source: Michael Pinto-Duschinsky, *British Political Finance 1830–1980* (American Enterprise Institute, 1982) and 'Trends in British political funding 1979–83', *Parliamentary Affairs*, vol. 38 no. 3, 1985, pp. 328–47. See also his article in *The Times*, 30 November 1992.

general elections the law is, in large measure, obeyed, even though enforcement is left to a petition by a defeated candidate and there has been no such challenge for overspending since 1929. In hotly fought by-elections, however, substantial breaches of the limit long went unchallenged and in 1989 the ceiling for by-elections was raised to four times the normal level.

Most parties spend near to the ceiling in constituencies they regard as marginal. However, since the average maximum in 1992 was a little over £7,000 (and, in most cases, only 25,000 or so votes are needed for victory), the amount remained quite modest and relatively easy to raise.

The cost to the state is hard to assess. In 1992 the expenses

Table 8.2 Average expenditure per candidate, 1900–1992

	Cash (£)			At 1980 prices (£)		
Year	Con	Lab	Lib/Alln	Con	Lab	Lib/Alln
1900	930	463	868	26,300	24,547	13,094
1945	780	595	532	7,534	5,138	5,747
1964	790	751	751	3,910	3,717	2,866
1979	2,190	1,897	1,013	2,543	2,218	1,184
1987	4,400	3,900	3,400	2,880	2,552	2,226
1992	5,840	5,090	3,169	3,000	2,614	1,628

Source: Adapted from M. Pinto-Duschinsky, *British Political Finance 1830–1980*
(American Enterprise Institute, 1982) and 'Trends in British political funding
1979–83', *Parliamentary Affairs*, vol. 38 no. 3, 1985, pp. 328–47.

claimed by returning officers amounted to more than £40m. A
further £28.5m had been spent on preparing the annual
electoral register. The services of the post office, with its free
delivery of mail, were probably worth about £10m. Security
arrangements for leading party figures was also costly.

The question whether campaigns should be subsidized from
taxation, as they now are in most Western democracies, was
raised by a government-appointed committee under Lord
Houghton in 1976.[1] It recommended substantial subsidies
both for routine party activities and for campaign costs. But its
proposals received a hostile reception from the Conservative
party and the press and were not followed up.

However, constituency campaigns have since 1918 received
a public subsidy through the free use of schools for meetings
and the right to one free postal delivery per elector. National
campaigns receive the major bonus of free time on radio and
television for party election broadcasts.

The only instance of direct cash payments towards the cost
of campaigning being authorized by parliament came with the
1975 referendum on membership of the European Economic
Community when £125,000 each was paid to the pro- and anti-
market umbrella organizations. The subsidy was designed to

prevent the pro-marketeers from seeming to have too grotes-
que a monetary advantage (in the event they spent £1,482,000
to the anti-marketeers' £134,000).

In the Euro-elections of 1979 and 1984 there were substantial grants to the parties from the funds of the European
Parliament, both for pre-campaign activities and for the campaign itself. In 1984 the Conservatives received £2.8m in total,
Labour £1.0m and the Alliance £0.3 m. But there were no such
subsidies in the 1989 or 1994 Euro-elections.

Whether money makes much difference to election outcomes is open to question. A few MPs have spent far less than
the permitted maximum in their constituency campaigns without any observable impact on the outcome. There seems to be
little correlation between the amount of money spent on a party
election broadcast and the appreciation rating it achieves. It
has yet to be proved that press advertising, by far the most
expensive of campaign activities, has any impact on voting
preferences. Although the glossy packaging of the party
leaders' travels and 'photo-opportunities' during the final
weeks cost more and more in the 1980s, the sums are trivial
compared to the total advertising budget of recent elections.
Money can make most difference to the electoral fortunes of a
party when it is used to provide competent, well-paid staff
working over the years in party headquarters (above all in the
research and publicity departments).

None the less, the parties' need for money must affect their
conduct. Since 1967 companies have been required to disclose
their political contributions, just as trade unions have always
been. There is no evidence of any crude impropriety in the
relationship between the Conservatives and their main source
of funds, big business, or between the Labour party and the
trade unions. Despite the notorious boast at the 1952 Labour
Party Conference by Arthur Deakin of the Transport Workers
that 'he who pays the piper calls the tune', threats to withdraw
party contributions over specific policy decisions have not
loomed large in recent history. In so far as the Conservatives
act as the party of business and Labour as the party of the
unions, it is more due to a genuine coincidence of feeling and
interest than to any financial influence.

Note

1 *Report* of the Committee on Financial Aid to Political Parties (London, HMSO, Cmnd 6601) 1976. See also the Hansard Society Report *Paying for Politics* (1981).

9 The National Campaign

The planning and nature of the national campaign have changed profoundly. In the early 1950s, once the manifesto had been prepared and launched, the main job of party headquarters was to arrange the leaders' tours and give their schedules and speeches to the press and to prepare and distribute literature. The party headquarters did send out daily notes to candidates and they had, of course, to cope with legal and administrative problems from the constituencies and regions as well as with occasional policy questions. They also had to coordinate the election broadcasts on radio, although these, being straight talks, were largely written by those who delivered them. In addition, party headquarters gathered in reports from the constituencies (which were often misleading) and passed them on to their leaders. The leading figures in each party did, to a very limited extent, talk to each other on the telephone. But, by modern standards, there was extraordinarily little intercommunication or discussion of strategy or tactics. The leaders proceeded, like juggernauts, on their pre-planned campaign tours, saying whatever they thought fit at their whistle-stops and at their grand evening rallies. The newspapers picked up whatever themes they fancied for their headline stories and these provided the main source of popular information about what was going on in the campaign.

The role of the party leader has, of course, been changed, principally by television. The alternative Prime Ministers must always be key figures in an election but the level of their prominence and their relationship to the party machine can be very variable. The speeches of Mr Churchill and Mr Attlee in 1945, 1950 and 1951 were dutifully reported in the press but there is no evidence of their being involved in day-to-day strategic discussion; they did not need the elaborate briefing and preparation that daily press conferences and television interviews, with all their pitfalls, require. They stood on their party manifesto and made only occasional references to the utterances of the other side. It was the same for Sir Anthony Eden in 1955 and even, to some extent, for Harold Macmillan and Hugh Gaitskell in 1959, although 1959 was certainly the turning point.

Who runs elections? Ostensibly, the party campaigns are managed from party headquarters, in Smith Square, by the Conservative party chairman or in Walworth Road (though in Smith Square, too, up to 1979) by the general secretary of the Labour party. In practice, a wide variety of command structures has been employed and very often there has been great strain between the officials at the centre and the party leaders and their entourage. As parties have become more sophisticated and self-conscious about strategy and about propaganda techniques, the advertising consultants, the professional organizers and the politicians have found increasing difficulty in coordinating their activities without friction. From the bypassing of Morgan Phillips by Dick Crossman and his campaign committee in 1959 to the spectacular and well-leaked tensions between Margaret Thatcher and Norman Tebbit during the 1987 Conservative campaign, there have been many instances of confusion. In 1987 John Pardoe, who chaired the Alliance campaign committee, complained that David Owen and David Steel time and again went against agreed decisions: 'the campaign was the greatest disappointment of my life'. None the less, every party has developed an increasingly comprehensive planning structure, a 'war book' agenda for each day of the campaign, and a regular forum for information-gathering and for strategic decision-making. Often there is little that can be done to change course. The campaign develops its own momentum and it becomes increasingly difficult to control what tired politicians do and say, or to prevent excited and frustrated advisers from revealing more than they should to reporters.

In the last resort, however, control does now rest with the party leaders for it is they who, on television and at press conferences, are carrying the party message. Martin Harrison has calculated that during the 1987 election out of 2,823 references to politicians' speeches in national radio and television news bulletins 1,454 (53 per cent) were to party leaders and only 47 per cent to secondary party figures. And in 1992 at least the party leaders were consulted on all national advertising copy; when the leaders were on tour, the headquarters in London tried to keep in constant touch by telephone to seek authority for any significant statement they wished to issue at short notice. But party leaders always have their own private team of secretaries and cronies who may or may not be in tune with headquarters. Friction is inevitable and the media have become more intrusive and more skilled at detecting any tensions.

All evolution is gradual. Each election differs from its predecessor, and most of the developments that are seized on as new have their roots in previous contests. But the 1959 campaign does stand out from all the rest, with features that became standard in subsequent elections making their first significant appearance. The Conservatives initiated large-scale advertising during the election run-up (see p. 111). The Labour party made press conferences a major campaign feature and exploited private polls (see p. 117). Most important of all, television came into its own as the main forum for the party battle (see p. 106).

The issues on which the parties wish to fight an election are still summarized in manifestos launched centrally by each party's headquarters and in addresses put out by the candidates in the constituencies. Manifestos usually open with a broad sweep of praise and condemnation, often in a special message from the leader. This has not changed much over the years as these excerpts from 1950 and from 1992 show:

1950 Labour *Let Us Win Through Together*

Britain has accomplished a recovery unsurpassed by any other country. No doubt there have been mistakes. But judge on what basis you will – by the standard of life of the general body of citizens, by employment, by the infrequency of serious industrial disputes, by the stability of the nation, by social security – by any fair comparisons, the British people have done an infinitely better job than was done after the first world war. By explaining to the people what needed to be done, by giving the facts, by appealing to the patriotism of the people, by vigorous, sensible leadership, the Labour Government has led Britain to the first victories of peace. Now let us win through together.

1950 Conservative *This is the Road*

From the time the Socialists acquired power they pretended that their policy was bringing the prosperity they had promised. They tried to make out that before they got a majority the whole history of Great Britain, so long admired and envied throughout the world, was dark and dismal. They spread the tale that social welfare is something to be had from the State free, gratis, and for nothing. They have put more money into circulation, but it has bought less and less. The value of every pound earned or saved or paid in pensions or social services has been cut by 3s. 8d. since they took office. It is not a pound but 16s. 4d.

1992 Conservative *The Best Future for Britain*

Only Conservatives can truly claim to be the party of opportunity, choice, ownership and responsibility. Socialists like to keep people under the government's thumb. Conservatives want to give them independence. But we want to put government at your service, giving you what you've paid for – good public services, responsible to you. You know I believe in choice and in this election, as always, there is

1992 Labour *Time to Get Britain Working Again*

Gripped by the longest recession since the war, Britain needs a government with a clear sense of direction and purpose. A government with the people and the policies to get Britain working again and to achieve sustained recovery – strength with staying power. Labour will be such a government.

A Conservative government would mean a repeat of the same stale policies which brought

94   The National Campaign

(*The Best Future for Britain*, continued)

(*Time to Get Britain Working Again*, continued)

another choice. You can vote for our opponents, and watch them take Britain back to the 1970s. Back to socialism. Back to strikes. Back to strife. Back to the world's pity, or worse still, contempt.

Under the Conservatives, Britain has regained her rightful influence in the world. We have stood up for the values our country has always represented. We have defended Britain's interests with vigour and with success. The respect with which Britain is regarded in the world has rarely been higher.

The 1990s present a great economic opportunity for Britain. We have got the scourge of inflation under control. We have cut direct tax rates. And a stable currency gives industry a chance to realise the potential released by the reforms of the 1980s.

We have extended ownership more widely – of homes, savings and shares – with millions more sharing directly in Britain's success. We will promote enterprise through low taxes, sound money and stable currency.

• We will aim to bring home ownership, share ownership and personal pensions within the reach of more families.

• We will continue to reform the taxation of savings, building on the success of Peps and Tessas.

economic insecurity, privatised and underfunded public services and increased social division. The Conservatives have no policies which would mean sustained recovery, higher health care or improved educational standards. The arrogance remains which brought us the poll tax, centralisation in Britain and isolation in Europe. If they can't get it right in 13 years, they never will.

The Labour government will mean a fresh start for Britain. It will mean strong and continued emphasis on investment for economic strength. It will mean action to help families, fair taxation, incentives for enterprise and support for essential community services. It will mean greater freedom, security and opportunity. It will mean change for the better.

It's time to make the change. It's time for Labour.

Britain's economic problems are deep-seated. We will not be able to do at once everything that we would like to do. But we will get down to business right away. And as with any properly run business, our immediate programme will be part of a strategy for long-term success.

Every action we propose makes sense by itself. Together, our proposals add up to a co-

(*The Best Future for Britain*, continued)

- We will raise the tax threshold for inheritance tax so that the homes and savings of an increasing number of our citizens can pass unencumbered from one generation to another.

Some activities of government must always be provided in the public sector. But in central government, Next Steps agencies and local government, management is increasingly buying in services from the private sector. Our proposals for developing this policy have been set out in the white papers on *Competing for Quality* in central and local government.

- We will continue our privatisation programme. British Coal will be returned to the private sector. So will local authority bus companies. We will encourage local authorities to sell their airports. We will end British Rail's monopoly. We will sell certain rail services and franchise others.

The Citizen's Charter is the most far-reaching programme ever devised to improve quality in public services. It addresses the needs of those who use public services, extends people's rights, requires services to set clear standards – and to tell the public how far those standards are met.

(*Time To Get Britain Working Again*, continued)

ordinated programme for recovery.

By investing in house-building and repairs, we start to rehouse homeless people.

By investing in public transport, we start to transform commuters' lives and create a cleaner environment.

By investing in the NHS, we offer new security to the patients and the public.

By investing in educating, we nourish the talents of children and lay the basis for future success.

Business needs sustained and balanced growth, stable exchange rates and low inflation. We will deliver them.

This election will decide the future of the NHS. Indeed, it will decide whether or not we continue to have a NHS of the kind that the British people want.

The Conservatives would continue to commercialise and privatise the NHS until it is run as just another business. With Labour, it will be modernised and returned as a high-quality public service, accountable to the community.

Our charter of rights, backed up by a complementary and democratically enforced bill of rights, will establish in law the specific rights of every citizen.

But the glittering generalities of such opening paragraphs have always been followed by specific promises and expositions of policy covering several thousand words.

Parties continue to put great efforts into their election manifestos. These documents, though widely circulated, are little read. But they are very important, first because rash promises or internal contradictions will be seized on by the other side and exploited as evidence of the party's unfitness to govern and, secondly, because the manifesto is treated as a promissory note. The Civil Service prepares briefs on how the policies are to be carried out; the House of Lords accepts that it must not frustrate the enactment of a specific manifesto pledge endorsed by a clear election result; and party activists cite the manifesto in attempts to prevent their pragmatic leaders from backsliding. It was only because steel nationalization was included in the 1945 manifesto that a reluctant Labour Cabinet went ahead with legislation in 1948. In 1964 the Conservatives boasted that they had carried out 93 of the 94 explicit commitments in their 1959 manifesto.

Much is said about the mandate conferred by an election. The victor is supposed to be authorized, even obliged, to carry out the promises made during the campaign – and if they later decide to do something that they did not then mention, they can be accused of having no mandate for their action. The idea that an election should be treated as a set of binding referendums on each and all of the policies put forward by the rival parties is somewhat absurd. But there is much to be said for the idea that there should be some moral and political pressure on politicians, first to exercise prudence in making promises and, secondly, to keep them when made. So the fiction of the mandate has its value.

Manifestos have tended to be long and usually turgid catalogues of policies in relation to all major issues. Governments usually point with pride to past achievements but are inhibited by the fact of being the party in power from referring to shortcomings or offering major new initiatives, although the Conservatives' 1983 promise to abolish the Greater London Council and the Metropolitan counties and their 1987 promise to introduce a poll tax in place of domestic rates stand out as exceptions to that proposition. Oppositions have an easier task in pointing to the deficiencies of the past few years and suggesting alternative policies.[1]

The election addresses of candidates offer some guide to the central areas of argument. Many issues recur, election after election. Unemployment, prices, pensions, the health service and housing all received mention in a majority of election addresses over the past 45 years. Nationalization, a leading theme in the 1950s, was referred to by less than 5 per cent of Conservative or Labour candidates in 1987. Imperial and Commonwealth issues disappeared in the 1960s with the end of Empire. Immigration only featured significantly during the 1960s. Agriculture, always a minority theme, was noticed by less than one candidate in 12 in 1987. But law and order, hardly mentioned in the 1950s, was referred to by over two-thirds of all candidates in 1987. And socialism was barely mentioned by Labour candidates.

The personality of party leaders varied in the extent to which it was thought to have appeal. Among 1959 Conservatives 65 per cent mentioned Harold Macmillan, while in 1983 56 per cent of Conservatives mentioned Margaret Thatcher (though only 17 per cent did so in 1987). Michael Foot, with 1 per cent in 1983, was the least acknowledged of Labour leaders (47 per cent of 1966 Labour addresses referred to Harold Wilson).

The Labour party used to be much exercised by the fear of election scares. Three inter-war contests had left their memories or their myths. There was the 1918 contest, with its arbitrary 'coupon' for those endorsed by Lloyd George and with the shrill slogans 'Hang the Kaiser' and 'Homes fit for heroes'. But it was the Zinoviev letter alarum in 1924 and the Savings Bank scare in 1931 that really made their mark; they came to be remembered as excuses for Labour's defeats following its first two periods in office. In 1945 and 1950 the Labour party put considerable effort into immunizing the electorate against some unforeseen Tory scare. In fact, these have never materialized on any serious scale. If anything, the Conservative complaints about Labour exploitation of the warmonger theme in 1951 come nearest to the classic idea of a scare. Elections campaigns have been slightly knocked off course by particular news stories (the Gaitskell tax pledge in 1959, the British Oxygen strike in 1964, the trade statistics in 1970, the Figgures figures in February 1974), but in the whole of the post-war period it would be hard to point to a decisive reward for an unscrupulous initiative, or a spontaneous rumour, from any quarter.

Parties are constantly challenged to take up particular issues such as environmentalism, feminism, gay rights, black rights or animal welfare. In practice, many of these are marginal or counter-productive in their impact on the middle-of-the-road elector whose vote is being sought. But if the issue has any mileage and excites little enmity, all parties will take it up. It used to be the tragedy of the moderate, reasonable Liberals that if they produced a worthwhile new policy, one or both of the big parties would steal it; it was very hard to maintain a distinct set of proposals which were unacceptable to the moderate right or the moderate left.

And from 1950 to the mid-1970s a Butskellite mood of consensus prevailed; despite the rhetoric of confrontation in parliament, there was far-reaching agreement between the parties over key issues. But after Labour's defeat in 1979 a wider gap developed, and in 1983 fundamental disagreements were voiced between Conservative and Labour over Europe, over defence, over union policy and over privatization. However in 1987 and even more in 1992 an underlying consensus could be detected.

The issues that are formally raised in manifestos or in the course of a campaign can be important not just for their immediate impact on votes (which is usually very limited) but for their long-term significance in shaping the discourse of politics. It has been suggested that campaigns do not decide the current election so much as the subsequent one; for example, Labour's failure in 1955 can be attributed to the proving false of the party's 1951 themes: that a Tory victory threatened unemployment, the dismantling of the welfare state and even, in the last resort, war.

If an issue is to have an impact on votes it must satisfy each of three conditions: (a) the electorate must have strong feelings about it (if they don't mind much, their votes won't move); (b) the electorate must have a one-sided approach (if they are equally divided, any stance will alienate as many as are attracted); and (c) the electorate must genuinely perceive a sharp contrast between the party stances (if, as so often, the parties' positions are not clearly differentiated in the public mind, their stance will have little effect). Remarkably few issues satisfy all these three conditions fully enough to have much effect on election outcomes.

Furthermore, the issues that parties talk about are not necessarily the issues that decide votes. But they are, in general, the issues that voters say are important. Pollsters seldom uncover any theme prominent in the voters' minds that has been ignored by the politicians. However, issues that have certainly been of national importance have sometimes been excluded from serious electoral debate; the atom bomb and immigration in the 1950s and entry into Europe in the 1960s provide outstanding examples.

The declaration of the election results has always provided a dramatic national occasion. In 1945, because of the need to wait for the votes of servicemen overseas, the count was delayed for three weeks until 9 a.m. on Thursday 26 July. But then news of the astonishing overturn of Winston Churchill came quickly; Labour won three-quarters of the 250 seats declared by lunchtime. At 7 p.m. Churchill went to the Palace to resign and Clement Attlee was then summoned to form a government. Despite the unexpectedness of the result, the transition was effected smoothly. By the next day, Attlee had announced his main Cabinet members and he and Ernest Bevin were on their way to Potsdam to replace Churchill and Eden at the Summit Conference with Roosevelt and Stalin.

In 1950 the polls closed at 9 p.m. on 23 February. About half the seats were counted on the night. It was the first election to have the results reported on television and, as the programme was scheduled for 10.45 p.m., it started dramatically with the first result which came in unexpectedly early. However, because of the closeness of the outcome (Labour won by five seats), it was not plain until late on the following afternoon that Labour would be back with a majority.

In October 1951 the routine was similar but this time the

margin was slightly larger. At 5 p.m. on the Friday, as soon as the Conservatives won the 313th seat that gave them a clear majority, Clement Attlee drove to the Palace to resign and by 5.30 p.m. Winston Churchill was again Prime Minister.

Over the elections that followed more and more seats counted on the Thursday night, until by 1987 599 out of 650 did so. The trend of the results became clear earlier and earlier. In October 1964 430 constituencies declared overnight and it seemed plain from the start that Labour was going to oust the Conservatives. But the party fared less well in the later results and it was not until 3 p.m. on the Friday that the clear majority was announced. Sir Alec Douglas-Home then resigned and Harold Wilson became Prime Minister. On 18 June 1970 the position was reversed. Labour's setback was plain from the first result but Wilson did not concede until the following midday. At 2.15 p.m. on 19 June the 316th Conservative victory was announced but Wilson could not resign until the Queen had driven back to Buckingham Palace from the race meeting at Ascot.

On Thursday 28 February 1974 it was certain from the overnight returns that no clear majority was likely. Edward Heath did not in fact resign until 6.30 p.m. the following Monday when it had become certain that the Conservatives could not secure Liberal or Ulster Unionist support.

The 1979 election offers the speediest example of a transfer of power. The outcome was plain from the outset and at 2.30 p.m. on Friday 4 May Jim Callaghan went to the Palace to make way for Margaret Thatcher.

Each of the six transfers of power brought about by post-war elections has taken place swiftly and smoothly. Only in March 1974 was there a three-day hiccup, as the political situation was sorted out. But the Civil Service, so often called the permanent government of Britain, and in particular the Cabinet Secretary and the staff at No. 10, have always had contingency plans ready. No incoming Prime Minister has complained about the capacity of public servants to cope with these inordinately rapid upheavals. In almost every other democracy a few days or even weeks are allowed to elapse. The arrival of removal vans in Downing St before all the counts are complete has no parallel elsewhere. The advantages of this extreme haste are not immediately apparent.

Note

1 See I. Budge, 'Manifestos and mandates', *Contemporary Record*, vol. 1 no. 4, 1987, and his article in *The Financial Times*, 23 October 1987.

10 The Media

The press has always been partisan. With a very few exceptions, it has been the custom for newspapers to give clear
advice to their readers on how to vote, and in almost all cases
this editorial opinion has influenced the coverage of news
throughout the campaign.

The positions and circulation of national daily newspapers
since the war have been concisely summarized by Colin
Seymour-Ure. Table 10.1, based on his work, shows the
circulation and partisanship of the London-based newspapers
which, throughout the period, have reached into between 70
and 85 per cent of all the households in Britain. In 1987 almost
half of all morning daily sales were cornered by two newspapers, the *Sun* and the *Daily Mirror*, both totally partisan,
although on opposite sides, and neither of them making any
serious attempt at full reporting even of their own side.

The press has played an important part in every election in
providing information for the voters and, to some degree, in
setting the agenda for the campaign. Newspapers report politicians and political activity. Journalists are stimulated – and
sometimes manipulated – by the politicians. But they in turn
also stimulate – and sometimes manipulate – the politicians.

However, their activities have changed. Up to 1959, because
of the self-abnegation of the BBC, they had a monopoly on the
news: for most people there was no other way of knowing about
the events of the campaign. Snippets from speeches formed the
staple of reporting, even in the tabloids. But from 1959
onwards it was different. The evening broadcasts would pick

The Sun and *Daily Mirror* front-page headlines on election day, Thursday 9 June 1983.

up anything notable said during the day. The morning press took more to sensation-hunting and side-issues; gimmick photographs, opinion polls, personal gossip, verbal stumbles and local scandals became the normal fare of the tabloids: serious balanced reporting became increasingly neglected. For the quality press articles about broad themes and about campaign strategy and about psephology took a larger and larger share of the space; the coverage became increasingly sophisticated and analytic but the politicians complained that their speeches were less than ever covered.

The parties have become increasingly interested in, and skilled at, influencing the content of the press. The coming of full formal daily London press conferences in 1959 meant that news was made centrally at party headquarters and not in evening speeches in distant cities. The desired messages were sent to Fleet Street early in the day. The top journalists were able to question the top politicians without having to travel the country. And, as the politicians learnt the need to provide good visual material for television, they offered a rich spin-off for press photographers, with striking pictures of themselves against

Table 10.1 Circulation (in thousands) and partisanship of national daily newspapers in general elections, 1945–1992

	1945	1950	1951	1955	1959	1964	1966	1970	1974F	1974O	1979	1983	1987[a]	1992
Daily Herald/Sun[b]	1,850 Lab	2,030 Lab	2,003 Lab	1,759 Lab	1,465 Lab	1,300 Lab	1,274 Lab	1,509 Lab	2,966 Con	3,152 Coalition	3,942 Con	4,155 Con	3,993 Con	3,571 Con
Daily Mirror	2,400 Lab	4,603 Lab	4,514 Lab	4,725 Lab	4,497 Lab	5,085 Lab	5,019 Lab	4,850 Lab	4,291 Lab	4,256 Lab	3,783 Lab	3,267 Lab	3,127 Lab	2,903 Lab
Daily Express	3,300 Con	4,099 Con	4,169 Con	4,036 Con	4,053 Con	4,190 Con	3,987 Con	3,670 Con	3,290 Con	3,255 Con	2,458 Con	1,936 Con	1,697 Con	1,525 Con
Daily Mail	1,704 Con	2,215 Con	2,267 Con	2,068 Con	2,071 Con	2,400 Con	2,464 Con	1,938 Con	1,730 Con	1,762 Con	1,973 Con	1,834 Con	1,759 Con	1,673 Con
Daily Star	–	–	–	–	–	–	–	–	–	–	880 Neutral	1,313 Con	1,289 Con	806 None
Daily Telegraph	813 Con	984 Con	998 Con	1,055 Con	1,181 Con	1,324 Con	1,337 Con	1,391 Con	1,419 Con	1,421 Con	1,358 Con	1,284 Con	1,147 Con	1,038 Con
(Manchester) Guardian	83 Lab	141 Lib	139 Lib/Con	156 Lib/Con	183 Lab/Lib	278 Lab	270 Lab/Lib	297 Lab/Lib	346 Con/Lab Lib balance	356 More Lib influence Lab	275 Lab	417 Not Con landslide	494 Lab	429 Lab

Independent	–	–	–	–	–	–	–	–	–	–	–	–	293 None	390 None
The Times	204 Neutral	258 Con	232 Con	222 Con	254 Con	255 Con	254 More Lib	414 Con/Lib	345 Con/Lib	348 Con/Lib	Not published	321 Con	442 Con	386 Con
News Chronicle	1,549 Lib	1,525 Lib	1,507 Lib	1,253 Lib	1,207 Lib	–	–	–	–	–	–	–	–	–
Daily Sketch/ Daily Graphic[c]	896 Con	777 Con	794 Con	950 Con	1,156 Con	847 Con	844 Con	839 Con	–	–	–	–	–	–
Total circulation	12,799	16,632	16,623	16,224	16,067	15,679	15,449	14,908	14,387	14,550	14,669	14,527	14,544	12,721
Total Conservative circulation[d]	6,713 (52%)	8,333 (50%)	8,599 (52%)	8,487 (52%)	8,725 (54%)	9,016 (57%)	8,632 (56%)	8,252 (55%)	9,750 (68%)	6,786 (47%)	9,731 (66%)	10,843 (75%)	10,327 (71%)	8,193 (64%)
Total Labour circulation[d]	4,454 (35%)	6,633 (40%)	6,517 (39%)	6,484 (40%)	6,145 (38%)	6,663 (42%)	6,563 (43%)	6,656 (44%)	4,291 (30%)	4,256 (29%)	4,058 (28%)	3,267 (22%)	3,617 (25%)	3,332 (26%)

[a] In 1987 there were two new papers: The Independent (293, Neutral) and Today (307, Coalition). (1992 The Independent [390, Neutral], Today [533, Con])

[b] Financial Times and Daily Worker/Morning Star omitted. The Sun replaced the Daily Herald in 1964.

[c] Named Daily Graphic 1946–52.

[d] Includes papers with divided support.

Sources: C. Seymour-Ure, The Political Impact of the Mass Media (Constable, 1974), table 6.1; Nuffield election studies.

surprising backgrounds or in unusual clothes. Moreover, the specialists at party headquarters put increasing effort into monitoring the press and feeding good copy to sympathetic editors or reporters. There are limits to this sort of manipulation but there is no doubt that it has been greatly on the increase in the past few elections.

Undoubtedly, the press remains very important. A majority of voters still sees a daily newspaper and, even though many may jump over the political stories, they cannot totally shut out the headlines. Moreover, newspapers continue to influence the agenda of the campaign. Political news in the press may have a diminishing direct impact on the voters, but it is analysed ever more exhaustively at party headquarters and in television news rooms. The politicians, the journalists at the press conferences, the television interviewers and the television editors all read the papers and react to any stories they see as significant. The judgements of the commentators about how the campaign is going feed back to the party strategists and help to shape their decisions.

The evolution of political broadcasting, however, has done more to transform elections than any other development in the past 40 years. From 1945 to 1955 party broadcasts were the BBC's only contribution to the contest (see table 10.2) and the BBC had a monopoly of broadcasting. But from 1959 onwards elections became the most important of all challenges to the broadcasters. Television, which had only just achieved comprehensive national coverage, both in the BBC and the com-

Table 10.2 Number of party election broadcasts, 1945–1955

Year	Radio			Television		
	Con	Lab	Lib	Con	Lab	Lib
1945	10	10	4	–	–	–
1950	5	5	3	–	–	–
1951	5	5	3	1	1	1
1955	4	4	1	4	4	1

mercial service, reported the campaign in detail and devoted most of its current affairs programmes to reports and arguments on specific issues. Radio, with its diminished audience, followed suit. By the time of the 1964 election, two-thirds of the population said that they derived most of their political information from television and since then the primacy of television has increased. The parties have planned their campaigns more and more exclusively to secure the maximum impact on the television screen. The 'media events' and 'photo-opportunities' which are now fitted daily into every leader's schedule excite cynical comment but they none the less serve their purpose. Television wants pictures far more than words and the politicians have shown increasing ingenuity in supplying them; it is very difficult for news editors to resist colourful shots, even when they show non-events.

Another impact of broadcast coverage has come with the lengthening of the newsmakers' day. Lunchtime bulletins in the 1970s and breakfast television in the 1980s mean that four or five times in every 24 hours the broadcasters are seeking a fresh headline story to top their bulletin. A story has to be a very strong one, with several ramifications, for it to lead the news from morning till night. Therefore the parties tempt the broadcasters with fresh copy, and it is hard to keep any issue, however important, in the forefront long enough for its significance to be fully explored. It is arguable that the speeding up of campaigns, induced by television, has had the effect of trivializing them.

In the 1950s the politicians were frightened of television. Harold Macmillan described the moments before appearing as worse than waiting to go over the top in the trenches in 1916. Television performances were stilted and formal. The first breakaway was in 1959 when Labour imitated the *Tonight* formula of the BBC's daily current affairs programme, although for a while the 'head and shoulders' style of talking straight to camera continued. But the techniques, first of the film documentary, and then of the television commercial, gradually took hold. In the 1975 referendum, the Britain-in-Europe campaign employed an American expert, Charles Guggenheim with his *ciné-verité* expertise, to make their four programmes. And in 1987, Hugh Hudson, famous as a film producer, prepared the brilliant biographical puff of Neil Kinnock which sent his rating as a leader soaring (though it did not have the same impact on the Labour party's poll support).

How many election broadcasts each party should have has been a source of controversy, above all because the ratio of party broadcasts is used as a guide to the allocation of time in news and other programmes. The Liberals attributed their regular upsurges during the campaign to their increased exposure and the third party has, as table 10.3 shows, moved up to equality with Conservative and Labour.

The amount of party broadcasting has, in fact, diminished because the programmes are shorter. Since 1966 none has lasted more than ten minutes, compared to the half-hour talks common up to 1955. The brevity of the public's attention span has been increasingly recognized; indeed, in 1983 the Conservatives voluntarily renounced five minutes of their ten-minute broadcasts on the ground that a shorter message was more effective.

Such an attitude may also reflect the diminishing importance attached to party broadcasts. Items in the news and long interviews with the leaders in other programmes are now recognized as far more important. The propagandist and self-advertising quality of party broadcasts can even be counter-productive.

Yet there is no doubt that television has become the prime

Table 10.3 Number of party election broadcasts, 1959–1992

	Radio			Television		
Year	Con	Lab	Lib Dem	Con	Lab	Lib Dem
1959	8	8	2	5	5	2
1964–74F	7	7	4	5	5	3
1974O–79	7	7	5	5	5	4
1983	7	7	6	5	5	4
1987	7	7	7	5	5	5
1992	7	7	7	5	5	4

source of electoral communication. The leader has become ever more important in carrying the party's message as each news bulletin gives its balanced few minutes to each contender. Since there always has to be a camera crew accompanying each party leader, and the leader's handlers make sure there is some good photo-copy, the leaders always appear – leaving limited time for anyone else.

Broadcasting has changed the language of politics. The exaggerated rhetoric, traditional on the hustings and in parliament, is recognized as quite inappropriate when a politician intrudes, uninvited, into the nation's sitting rooms. Views are expressed more moderately, even in face-to-face confrontations, and the voters are made aware how much politicians have in common with each other, both in opinions and in character. It is far harder to see either side as angels or as devils after continuous exposure to them on the screen. The increased volatility of the electorate over the past quarter of a century is due more than anything to the new type of political education that television has offered to the British public.

11 Advertising and Polls

Casual travellers about Britain during recent general elections would have seen very little evidence of the campaign, unless they encountered the odd loudspeaker van or the very occasional motorcade. The use of posters, which were once much in evidence, declined sharply with the restraints on fly-posting imposed by the Town and Country Planning Act of 1947 and with the increased cost of major sites, which are, in any case, in short supply and usually tied up by long-term contracts. The Conservatives printed nearly 10,000 hoarding size posters in 1951 but less than 3,000 in 1970. Moreover, the advent of party labels on the ballot paper under the 1969 Act removed one traditional rationale for posters which used often to be designed simply to remind voters that 'Smith equals Conservative', 'Jones equals Labour', in order to prevent them making any mistake when it came to marking their crosses. However, in most parts of the country a tradition of displaying window-bills survives. Election addresses are usually designed so that they can be pasted up in supporters' front windows. After the 1987 election the Gallup poll reported that 12 per cent of voters said they had put up a window-bill for their party. Only 10 per cent made such a claim in 1970.

Large posters have, however, been used extensively outside the actual election period when there could be no serious question of contravening the law on constituency expenses. The most memorable example was early in 1959 when the Conservatives, intent on restoring their fortunes after Suez, launched a massive nine-month campaign based on the slogan

'Life's better with the Conservatives. Don't let Labour ruin it' beneath a huge photo of a happy family with the new consumer durables – car, refrigerator and television – in the background. There have been a number of poster campaigns since then but hardly on the same scale or with the same impact; in some cases parties have put up isolated posters for news photographers, to convey through television and the press a new slogan and to suggest a major campaign. In 1978 the Conservatives' agency, Saatchi and Saatchi, devised a £200,000 knocking campaign which included one powerful poster 'Labour isn't working' purporting to show a long dole queue. This survived to haunt the Conservatives, since in the next four years unemployment doubled under their rule. But in 1992 the parties decided that poster advertising during the campaign was legal as long as it was nationwide and not directed at marginal constituencies, and as long as it did not refer to individual candidates. The Consrvatives spent £1.5m. on 4,500 48-sheet poster sites, and the Labour party £0.5m. on 2,200 sites. It made the election appreciably more visible than any other since the war.

Press advertising has become increasingly important. It used

Conservative and Labour advertising campaign posters in 1959.

Conservative and Labour advertising campaign posters in 1979 and
1987 respectively.

to be thought illegal during campaigns. But a test case after the
1951 election opened the door to massive expenditure in this
area. The Tronoh-Malayan Tin Company had spent a few
hundred pounds during the campaign on publicizing a company report which attacked the evils of socialism: the Court
ruled that, since no person or party was named, it did not fall
under the prohibition on unauthorized expenditure designed
to promote the election of a candidate.

More than two years before the 1959 election the Conservatives launched a long-run series of advertisements in
the Sunday papers designed to remove the image of the
Conservatives as the party of a privileged minority. 'You're
looking at a Conservative' was the caption over pictures of a
cloth-capped, lumber-yard hand or a working-class woman,
as well as of famous figures from the world of sport. At the
same time various industries threatened with nationalization
engaged in their own image-building advertising campaigns.
In the two years before the 1964 election the Conservatives
spent nearly a million pounds on advertising, two-thirds of it
on press advertising, lauding the government's achievements.

This key Conservative advertisement in the 1979 campaign returned to haunt them as unemployment doubled in the next four years.

LABOUR'S POLICY ON ARMS.

CONSERVATIVE ☒
THE NEXT MOVE FORWARD

The Conservatives regarded this attack on Labour's policy of uni-
lateral disarmament as their best advertisement in the 1987 campaign.

Private enterprise (and in particular the steel industry) spent
a further million, attacking nationalization. On the other
side, Labour also engaged in some, more modest, press
advertising.

Uncertainty about the law for a long time deterred the
parties from press advertising in the final three weeks before
the poll. It was not until 1979 that it was used on a large scale
(though Liberal experiments in 1974 had paved the way). The
Conservatives spent £500,000 in the national press, mainly in
the last five days, while Labour spent £175,000 and the
Liberals £25,000.

In 1983 a new level was reached. In a period of three weeks
the Conservatives took a total of 67 pages in advertisements in
national papers; the Labour party took 27; the Alliance took
none. The Conservatives spent over £1.2m and Labour over
£0.4m.

In 1987 expenditure on advertising increased still further.
In the last four days of the campaign the Conservatives bought
11 full pages of advertising in almost every national paper,
completely overshadowing Labour's more modest effort and
perhaps helping to avert the last-minute slippage so fre-
quently suffered by the leading party. The Conservatives' total

bill for press advertising was about £3.6m compared to Labour's £1.6m.

There is, however, no solid evidence that press advertising justifies its enormous cost. When challenged, party officials and media advisers tend to say 'it's good for the morale of our own side' and 'if the others do it, we have to'. In the excitement of the final days of a campaign, no one can be certain that it will not make the critical difference. As the Conservative treasurer, explaining his lavishness in 1987, remarked: 'I'd rather be a poor party in office than a rich party in opposition'.

The 1945 general election was the first in Britain to be the subject of an opinion poll, when the Gallup poll reported a 47 per cent to 41 per cent lead for Labour over the Conservatives but, in the general ignorance about surveys, scant regard was paid to this forecast. In fact, Labour won by 48 per cent to 40 per cent.

Gallup had the field virtually to itself until 1959. Polls in the *Daily Express* and the *Daily Sketch* were not much regarded. But in 1959 three serious rivals appeared, and since then there have always been an array of polls competing for the best forecast. Until the mid-1960s newspapers tended to make their polls copyright and exclusive. Then it was realized that, while a poll was an expensive way of filling 20 column inches, it was a very cheap way of publicizing the sponsoring newspapers. The findings of every poll began to be released to rival journals and to the broadcast news bulletins for them to quote (with due attribution). This meant that a much more general awareness developed about the trends that the polls were uncovering.

The record of the polls as indicators of the result was relatively good until 1970 as Table 11.1 shows. Then a late swing to the Conservatives proved the general expectation of a Labour victory to be false. Only the Opinion Research Centre, adjusting its figures on the basis of the switches revealed in last-minute re-interviews with a few of its final sample, suggested a Conservative victory – and even then it underestimated Edward Heath's margin by 2 per cent. In February 1974 all the polls put the Conservatives ahead by just enough to give them a clear majority. In the actual outcome they led Labour by only 0.8 per cent in votes and were four seats behind them. In October 1974

Table 11.1 Polling error, 1945–1992

Year	Error on lead (%)	Error on party (%)	Number of polls
1945	3.6	1.6	1
1950	2.2	1.1	1
1951	4.0	1.5	1
1955	1.5	1.1	1
1959	1.8	1.2	2
1964	0.8	2.0	3
1966	2.1	1.0	3
1970	5.6	2.3	4
1974F	4.0	1.5	4
1974O	5.6	2.0	4
1979	2.4	1.3	3
1983	3.6	1.3	3
1987	4.0	1.6	4
1992	8.5	3.1	4

Mean difference between the actual results and the average estimate for
winning party's lead over second party and for average error on three major
party percentages in final polls by leading organizations.

all the polls overestimated Labour's margin by even more than
they had overestimated the Conservatives in February and a
predicted Labour landslide melted away to leave them with a
clear majority of just three seats.

After these misfortunes, the polls fared relatively well in the
clearcut elections of 1979, 1983, and 1987, only to meet their
worst disaster in 1992. After a campaign in which Labour was
ahead in 40 of the 50 nationwide polls, an average lead of 1 per
cent was reported on the morning of 9 April. The Conservatives emerged 7.5 per cent ahead and with a clear majority
of seats.

The reasons for the debacle were manifold – differential
refusal rates, differential turnout, omissions from the electoral
register, an outdated sample frame and some last-minute
switches seem each to have made a contribution.

But an error in one election will not prevent the media from sponsoring polls on the next. The popular press has to cover campaigns but finds much of the fine-gauge argument over issues to be boring. Yet the question 'who will win?' is never boring; polls can turn an election into a sporting event which will catch the public's fancy as much as speculation about the Grand National.

The record of the polls forecasting has been uneven, as table 11.1 shows. Under the 'cube law', an error of 2 per cent in the party lead meant an error of 36 in forecasts of the parliamentary majority, and even in the 1980s it would be equal to 18 or so seats.

The public is interested in polls mainly for their role in predicting how it, collectively, is going to vote. But there are other ways in which polls have changed elections and their interpretation. They show who votes in what way. Is Labour losing ground among skilled workers? Is the Alliance making special inroads among yuppies? Are women reacting differently to men? Polls also reveal where people stand on issues. Is Labour winning votes over the health service? Or losing them over defence? Which aspects of each party's appeal have most impact? And which are counter-productive?

Newspapers usually follow their voting predictions with brief reports on such questions, but these seldom make head-lines. They do, however, allow the public to set some of the election agenda, justifying journalists and television inter-viewers in focusing on the issues that worry electors even if politicians want to avoid them. Moreover, such findings are certainly studied in party headquarters and have a major effect on tactics, supplementing as they must the private opinion polls that have been conducted for the parties since the 1950s.

The Labour party arranged for some private polling in 1957–8, much to the disapproval of Aneurin Bevan who complained 'You are taking the poetry out of politics'. The Conservatives helped to set up the Opinion Research Centre in 1965, and since then they have sponsored extensive private research on issues and attitudes. From 1969 onwards the Labour party has employed Robert Worcester and his firm, Market and Opinion Research International (MORI).

Liberal and Alliance research has been more limited and spasmodic.

Evidence from private polls – and from public ones – has been used by both parties to deflate their own zealots, anxious to promote doctrinaire themes unlikely to have much positive appeal to the floating voter. They have also been used to test the acceptability of new approaches and new forms of words. The parties have become increasingly aware of the value of test-marketing their electoral appeal.

Yet the role of private polling should not be exaggerated. Most of the important findings about the electorate are generally available from public polls. The politicians, more-over, have their own convictions, as well as obligations to consistency and tradition, which limit their willingness (and indeed their freedom) to change course in the light of the latest poll findings. Private surveys have influenced the packaging of programmes and have had some impact on strategic priorities in the prominence given to particular issues. They were certainly important in 1983 and again in 1987 in giving Margaret Thatcher the assurance she needed when making her decision to call a summer election.

But during actual campaigns there have been very few occasions indeed when private poll findings have altered any party's strategy; one isolated example was the Labour decision to play the spectacular Kinnock-boosting television broadcast a second time during the 1987 campaign, when it was discovered how much the first showing had increased his rating and how few of the electorate had seen it. But, in so far as polls affect campaigns, it is mainly through the evidence they offer about voting intentions. This affects decisions on advertising expenditure and on the use of aggressive material: during the 1975 referendum the pro-marketeers, when they saw how easily they were winning, abandoned some abrasive advertising copy that linked the anti-marketeers with extremists.

But, above all, polls influence morale and tactics. Politicians do seem to campaign more effectively when they think they are winning. They also behave differently, depending on whom they see as their principal enemy. In the three-party politics of the 1980s, the Alliance campaign and its discussion of coalition possibilities depended critically on the trend of the Alliance's poll rating. The Conservatives, too, had alternative campaign emphases, which turned on how serious the Alliance threat seemed to be at the time.

Polls have certainly displaced canvass returns as a guide to each party on how it is doing in the country as a whole. Up to the 1950s the parties tried to make sense of the extraordinarily variable and unreliable evidence telephoned in by constituency agents, material which in 1945 convinced both sides that the Conservatives had won. Even at their worst, opinion polls are more reliable.

It is often asked whether polls affect the election result, either by inducing a bandwagon rush to the supposedly winning side or by encouraging underdog sympathy and a desire to temper the scale of victory. In 1967 the Speaker's Conference recommended a ban on polls during the campaign and in February 1987 a ten-minute rule Bill on the same theme received a first reading by 116 votes to 103 (the votes came mainly from Labour members, smarting from the Greenwich by-election in which polls seemed plainly to have induced Conservative votes to switch to the Alliance candidate in order to defeat Labour).

There is little solid evidence about the impact of polls. Until the 1960s they were too little remarked to have had much importance. It may be significant, however, that in seven successive elections from 1964 to 1983 the party that was ahead in the final surveys did in fact fare worse than had been predicted; the 1987 election was the only one since polls became fully disseminated when this underdog effect was absent.

However, it is plain that in 1987, if there had been only one poll as in 1945, and if it had been as little regarded as Gallup was then, the election would have been very different. Both the opposition parties would have been perceived on the basis of their meetings, press conferences and broadcasts to be more serious challengers to the Conservatives than in fact they were. The campaign could have had another shape – and so perhaps could the outcome. Party morale at headquarters and in the constituencies is shaped from day to day by the findings of the polls.

12 Local Electioneering

In the constituencies the routines of electioneering have continued largely unaltered since the war. About three weeks before the poll, the retiring MP or the prospective candidate is formally adopted by the local party. An election address is prepared and distributed by hand or by post to every household or every elector. The candidate's time is consumed by correspondence, by encountering the electorate in doorstep canvassing or street and marketplace walkabouts, by loudspeaker tours, and by meetings – sometimes small gatherings in private homes or as the guest of a church or society, sometimes at publicly advertised gatherings, usually on school premises. Meanwhile, the party workers are engaged in addressing envelopes and in canvassing. In theory, each home in the constituency should be visited in order to mark up every voter's preference on the electoral register; then on polling day, party tellers can tick off the names of supporters as they cast their ballots and chase up the laggards in the evening before the polling booths close.

Even in marginal seats, well organized by professional agents, this perfect model is seldom approached, and over much of the country there are now few public meetings and most electors are left uncanvassed. Parties do spend almost to the permitted maximum on printing leaflets and advertising but there are few places where there are enough party workers and enough organizing skills to carry out a really comprehensive campaign which can reach to every elector.

The major change over the past 40 years has been in the

decline in attendance at meetings and in the level of party activity. In 1951 30 per cent of electors claimed to have been to an election meeting; in 1992 only 1 per cent did so. In 1951 44 per cent said they were canvassed by the Conservatives and 37 per cent by Labour; in 1992 the figures were 12 per cent and 14 per cent. In 1950, almost every Conservative association and half the constituency Labour parties had a full-time paid agent. In 1992, Conservative full-time agents were half their 1950 number, while Labour had its own full timer in less than one seat in ten.

However, in the 1980s the official computerization of registers freed efficient parties from the soul-destroying routine of addressing envelopes to every voter and made possible more efficient monitoring of the canvassing process. The restraints on expenditure continued to limit exploitation of the American devices of local opinion polling, direct mail and telephonic soliciting of votes, as well as any extensive constituency advertising. But faxes and portable telephones led to more coordination of campaigning both within the constituency and between the national and local efforts.

Efforts to identify how much difference is made to the outcome by the quality of local organization have had little success. By and large, the relative uniformity of swing and turnout between adjacent constituencies, even with local parties of very different quality, spending different amounts of money, suggests that the routines of electioneering normally have little impact on the outcome; the very patchy and isolated successes of third parties must, however, owe a significant amount to the quality of the candidate and to the local organization.

13 Conclusion

Psephology, the academic study of elections, is a post-war phenomenon. The systematic recording of campaigns both as political processes and as moments in history, and the statistical analysis of results, despite some earlier echoes, really began in Britain with R. B. McCallum's pioneer venture, *The British General Election of 1945*. This has been followed by Nuffield College Studies of each subsequent general election which have moved in ever greater detail both into the *haute politique* of party strategy and into the exhaustive examination of the results.

But these books could not go into individual psychology or explain which people vote as they do: a sample survey approach is needed. Benney in London, and Milne in Bristol, together with their collaborators, studied voting behaviour in individual constituencies in the 1950s but it was not until the 1960s that a full-scale nationwide study was attempted with panel surveys before and after a series of elections. The British Election Survey has flourished since then, producing three major works, *Political Change in Britain* (covering 1963–70), *Partisan Dealignment in Britain* (1974–9) and *How Britain Votes* (1983). The raw material for these books has been re-analysed by other scholars to produce further books and articles.

At the same time the pollsters, in their published reports and in their private work for the parties, have contributed substantially to our knowledge about the demographic basis of party support and about the issues that stir voters. The serious press has produced more and more psephological reporting of quality.

Sir Lewis Namier described elections as locks on the river of British history, controlling the flow of events. Nowadays, elections have replaced the dates of monarchs as the historian's landmarks. But elections may decide less than they appear to. Certainly they decide less than is suggested in the rhetoric of campaign speeches. Consider the major landmarks of post-war British history:

1947	Convertibility crisis
1947	Independence of India and Pakistan
1948	Formation of NATO
1949	Devaluation
1950 (June)	Korean War
1956	Suez Crisis
1955–65	Successive decisions on decolonization
1961	The first attempt to enter Europe
1962	The pay pause
1967	The second attempt to enter Europe
1967	Devaluation
1972	The Northern Ireland crisis
1972	Entry into Europe
1976	The IMF crisis
1980	The Rhodesian settlement
1982	The Falklands War
1986	Single European Act
1990	Maastricht Treaty
1992	Leaving Exchange Rate Mechanism

None of these events was associated with an election. Most of them would have happened whichever party was in power – and in most cases any government would have reacted in the same way. The continuation in office or the changeover of power that followed each of the 13 post-war appeals to the country was not, in most cases, a vital determinant of national prosperity in the ensuing years. There would probably be general agreement that the most decisive change after 1945 was Margaret Thatcher's triumph in 1979. Certainly, its sequel, the 1983 election, in so far as it was between Conservative and Labour, offered the widest choice of any post-war contest. But many of the policies pursued in the 1980s have in fact reflected worldwide trends; what Margaret Thatcher has presided over in Britain has had its parallels under Labour governments in Australia and New Zealand.

But if the change, or the continuity, in party control that emerges from an election makes less difference than many suppose that does not mean that elections are unimportant, mere cosmetic devices to give legitimacy to the ruling cliques. The cynical left-wing comment 'If elections altered anything they'd abolish them' misses much of their significance. Barry Goldwater in the 1960s and Tony Benn in the 1980s could demand that elections should offer 'a choice, not an echo'. But if the choice in an election is too wide, if the victory of one side threatens too many of the population, a democratic system is bound to break down: people may take to the barricades rather than accept the verdict of the vote. Arthur Balfour said 'Democracy assumes that a nation is so fundamentally united that it can safely afford to bicker.' And parties that move too far from what the middle-of-the-road British can easily accept have, in fact, been punished at the polls.

But elections still play a major role in educating and influencing both electors and elected. In the three weeks of the campaign – and, for those most intimately involved, in the many months of preparation as well – people are educated about the issues facing the country. The manifestos that are prepared in a conscious pursuit of support, stressing the themes that do or should interest the voters, constitute agendas that will influence the conduct of government for years to come. And the rewards or punishments handed out by the election returns shape the careers and the thinking of those who rule or who aspire to rule the country.

The four-year rhythm of elections has a powerful effect on the conduct of ministers and opposition leaders. The detail and timing of policy-making does turn on election calendars and election outcomes.

What, then, do elections decide? Not, usually, 'the fate of the nation'. That is largely in the hands of social, technical and international trends that are beyond the control of any one government. But elections, and the shadow they cast before them, permeate the behaviour and the policy thinking of all politicians and all senior civil servants. What is thought to be acceptable to the voters conditions most of the decisions of Whitehall and Westminster. And election campaigns encapsulate what politicians can sell and what voters will buy.

But that leads to the reverse question. What decides elections? The great bulk of votes are predetermined by class, heredity, local environment and traditional loyalty. But an increasing proportion of the electorate does switch its support in response to specific issues or to an assessment of the likely performance in government of the rival contenders. And that assessment seems, above all, to be linked to the state of the economy and the perceived competence of the parties to handle it. But what constitutes the economy? There are many possible indicators of prosperity – real income, unemployment, rate of growth, balance of payments, level of taxation – and it is seldom that they all give the same message. The art of the politician lies in educating the public to respect whatever indicators are likely to be most favourable at the time when the next election comes. Thus, in the run-up to 1970 Harold Wilson stressed the balance of payments which, predictably, were coming right after two bleak years. In 1983 and 1987 the Conservatives stressed the fall in inflation, while Labour focused on the rise in unemployment. But in the last resort there is what the Australian Prime Minister, Ben Chifley, named as the ultimate determinant of elections, 'the hip-pocket nerve', the sense of being better-off or worse-off. Many other factors have come into the British electoral equation but, over the past half-century, this does appear to have loomed largest.

The function of elections is to record the decisions of individuals rather than to create them. The stir of the campaign induces people to go to the polling booths to register their pre-existing prejudices. Occasionally, the events of the final three weeks change enough hesitant minds to affect the outcome. And often the utterances of the campaign educate the voters and the participants to new expectations about what politics should yield over the coming years.

But the main impact of elections is in advance. Anxiety about the next election is the most universal of emotions among democratic politicians. Their actions are constantly shaped by their perceptions of what the public will stand. They cannot carry out the policies that they think the country needs or what their special interest groups desire, unless they win elections, and that means winning or retaining the support of a plurality of voters.

In the post-war period the Conservatives have been notably successful in this attempt. Although they have only won seven of the 14 general elections, they have won them all by viable majorities and therefore have been able to rule Britain for 31 of the 50 years since 1945. Labour won six times but only two of these victories were clear cut; three of the Labour parliaments were short-lived (and a fourth was paralysed by lack of a clear majority) so that Labour has had only 18 years in office and less than nine with full authority. The Conservative achievement, however, lies less in their length of tenure than in their success in containing and then driving back what they saw as the social- ist challenge. They reacted to their 1945 defeat by, over the next few years, accepting the welfare state and much of the Attlee government's achievement, and they edged their way back to office, with the help of the cumulative grievances inevitable in post-war austerity. They ruled for 13 years, while the country, though slipping back in the international league, added 50 per cent to its standard of living. Labour got back to power in 1964 and again in 1974 without any programme comparable to 1945 and each time economic difficulties drove the government off course; Labour accomplished some social and welfare reforms but it left few landmarks at which to point with pride. The Conservatives, too, went astray when they got back to office in 1970 and suffered from the perversities of the economy and the miners' strike.

But in 1979 luck and policy were with them. North Sea Oil, coming fully on stream, prevented the relative decline in the country's manufacturing base from turning into disaster. The economy grew and, despite appalling exceptions in some regions, most people became more prosperous. And the Con- servatives were fortunate politically. They had a strong and unchallenged leader. Their main adversary, the Labour party, turned in on itself, quarrelling, changing course and inducing the breakaway of the Social Democratic faction. Labour chose an inappropriate leader in Michael Foot and adopted policies that were unacceptable to much of middle Britain. In 1983 the party's vote plummeted to 28 per cent, their lowest share of the total since 1918 and their lowest vote per candidate since they were founded in 1900 (see figure 13.1). The party, with its roots in trade unionism, with council tenants and manual workers as its natural support, inevitably suffered as union membership fell, owner-occupation soared and manual workers dropped to less than half the working population. Despite vigorous efforts to adapt to the new world by Neil Kinnock and many of his colleagues, the Labour party had great difficulty in presenting itself as a convincing alternative government to an electorate when so many people, including its traditional supporters or their near relatives, had become house-owners, shareholders and white-collar workers. There were still many 'have-nots' but, now that the 'haves' were the majority, it was hard for Labour to retain its base, let alone advance from it.

For one or two brief moments it seemed that there was another serious challenge. Once or twice in 1981–2 and again in 1985–6 the Alliance topped the opinion polls; indeed, from 1981 to 1987 it secured more votes in by-elections than either of the other parties. But it had neither a strong power base in business or the unions, nor an entrenched body of habitual voters. Its MPs were too few to make much impact in parliament. Its support was too evenly spread for a breakthrough to be easy under the majoritarian electoral system; it came second in a majority of seats, but first in very few. So, despite getting a quarter of the electorate behind it, its impact on the political scene was limited. The Conservatives with only 42 per cent of the vote in four successive elections dominated the political scene in a way that looked like continuing.

But a glance at the history of the past 50 years cautions against such futurism. Few would have expected, five years before the event, the Labour triumph of 1945 or the Conservative return in 1951; to most people the general election outcomes in June 1970 and February 1974 were a complete surprise. But 1959 perhaps offers the greatest warning. Then, as in 1987, the Conservatives had won their third general election in a row; then, as in 1987, Labour was in disarray;

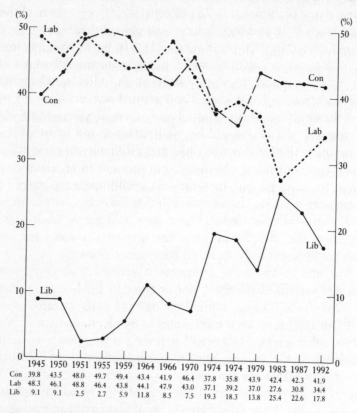

	1945	1950	1951	1955	1959	1964	1966	1970	1974	1974	1979	1983	1987	1992
Con	39.8	43.5	48.0	49.7	49.4	43.4	41.9	46.4	37.8	35.8	43.9	42.4	42.3	41.9
Lab	48.3	46.1	48.8	46.4	43.8	44.1	47.9	43.0	37.1	39.2	37.0	27.6	30.8	34.4
Lib	9.1	9.1	2.5	2.7	5.9	11.8	8.5	7.5	19.3	18.3	13.8	25.4	22.6	17.8

The moral of this figure can be seen more crudely by looking simply at the starting and finishing points of three lines in 1945 and 1992.

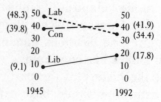

Figure 13.1 Voting trends, 1945–1992.

then, as in 1987, the economy seemed flourishing; then, as in 1987, there was a dominant successful Prime Minister. Three years later the Conservatives were floundering and in 1964 they lost office. In 1992 most people thought that a repeat of 1964 was coming. But against the odds, John Major snatched victory from the jaws of defeat – and then, before the year was out, sank to the lowest rating of any Prime Minister since the arrival of opinion polls.

The future does not always resemble the past and historic cycles are never exactly repeated. The study of elections reminds us of that truth as it chronicles how the techniques, the personnel and the subject matter of politics, though showing many continuities, can be transformed within the passage of a few years.

Year	Electorate (%) and turnout	Total votes cast	Conservative	Labour	Liberal (1983–7 Alliance)	Welsh and Scottish Nationalist	Communist	Others (mainly N. Ireland)
1945[a]	73.3% 32 836 419	100% (640) 24 082 612	39.8% (213) 9 577 667	48.3% (393) 11 632 191	9.1% (12) 2 197 191	0.2% 46 612	0.4% (2) 102 760	2.1% (20) 525 491
1950	84.0% 34 269 770	100% (625) 28 772 671	43.5% (299) 12 502 567	46.1% (315) 13 266 592	9.1% (9) 2 621 548	0.1% 27 288	0.3% 91 746	0.9% (2) 262 930
1951	82.5% 34 645 573	100% (625) 28 595 668	48.0% (321) 13 717 538	48.8% (295) 13 948 605	2.5% (6) 730 556	0.1% 18 219	0.1% 21 640	0.5% (3) 159 110
1955	76.8% 34 858 263	100% (630) 26 760 493	49.7% (345) 13 311 936	46.4% (277) 12 404 970	2.7% (6) 722 405	0.2% 57 231	0.1% 33 144	0.8% (2) 230 807
1959	78.7% 35 397 080	100% (630) 27 859 241	49.4% (365) 13 749 830	43.8% (258) 12 215 538	5.9% (6) 1 638 571	0.4% 99 309	0.1% 30 897	0.5% (1) 145 090
1964	77.1% 35 892 572	100% (630) 27 655 374	43.4% (304) 12 001 396	44.1% (317) 12 205 814	11.2% (9) 3 092 878	0.5% 133 551	0.2% 45 932	0.6% 169 431
1966	75.8% 35 964 684	100% (630) 27 263 606	41.9% (253) 11 418 433	47.9% (363) 13 064 951	8.5% (12) 2 327 533	0.7% 189 545	0.2% 62 112	0.7% (2) 201 032

1970	72.0% 39 342 013	100% (630) 28 344 798	46.4% (330) 13 145 123	43.0% (288) 12 178 295	7.5% (6) 2 117 033	1.3% (1) 381 818	0.1% 37 970	1.7% (5) 486 557
1974F	78.1% 39 770 724	100% (635) 31 340 162	37.8% (297) 11 872 180	37.1% (301) 11 646 391	19.3% (14) 6 058 744	2.6% (9) 804 554	0.1% 32 743	3.1% (14) 958 293
1974O	72.8% 40 072 971	100% (635) 29 189 178	35.8% (277) 10 464 817	39.2% (319) 11 457 079	18.3% (13) 6 346 754	3.5% (14) 1 005 938	0.1% 17 426	3.1% (12) 897 164
1979	76.0% 41 093 264	100% (635) 31 221 361	43.9% (339) 13 697 923	37.0% (269) 11 532 218	13.8% (11) 4 313 804	2.0% (4) 636 890	0.1% 16 858	3.2% (12) 1 043 755
1983	72.7% 42 197 344	100% (650) 30 671 136	42.4% (397) 13 012 315	27.6% (209) 8 456 934	25.4% (23) 7 780 949	1.5% (4) 457 676	0.04% 11 606	· 3.1% (17) 951 656
1987	75.3% 43 181 321	100% (650) 32 536 137	42.3% (376) 13 763 066	30.8% (229) 10 029 778	22.6% (22) 7 341 290	1.7% (6) 543 559	0.02% 6 078	2.6% (17) 852 368
1992	77.7% 43 249 721	100% 33 612 693	41.9% (376) 14 092 871	34.4% (271) 11 559 373	17.8% (20) 5 999 384	2.3% (7) 783 991	– –	3.5% (17) 1 176 692

Seats are shown in parentheses.

[a] The 1945 figures exclude university seats and are adjusted for double voting in the 15 two-member seats.

Source: D. Butler and D. Kavanagh, *The British General Election of 1992* (Macmillan, 1992).

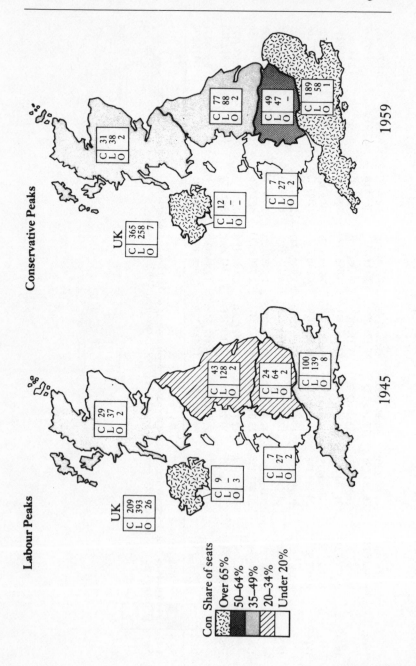

Conservative Peaks

C	31
L	38
O	2

C	77
L	88
O	2

C	49
L	47
O	–

C	189
L	58
O	1

C	7
L	27
O	2

C	12
L	–
O	–

UK
C	365
L	258
O	7

1959

Labour Peaks

C	29
L	37
O	2

C	43
L	128
O	2

C	24
L	64
O	2

C	100
L	139
O	8

C	7
L	27
O	2

C	9
L	–
O	3

UK
C	209
L	393
O	26

1945

Con Share of seats
Over 65%
50–64%
35–49%
20–34%
Under 20%

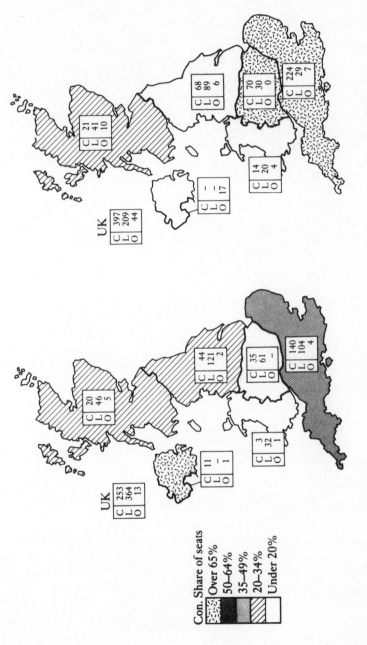

Con. Share of seats

- Over 65%
- 50–64%
- 35–49%
- 20–34%
- Under 20%

1966

UK	
C	253
L	364
O	13

C	20
L	46
O	5

C	11
L	–
O	1

C	44
L	121
O	2

C	35
L	61
O	–

C	3
L	32
O	1

C	140
L	104
O	4

1983

UK	
C	397
L	209
O	44

C	21
L	41
O	10

C	–
L	1
O	17

C	68
L	89
O	6

C	70
L	30
O	0

C	14
L	20
O	4

C	224
L	29
O	7

Bibliography

Alderman, G. *British Elections: Myth and Reality* (Batsford, 1978).

Benney, M., Pear, R. and Geiss, P. *How People Vote* (Routledge & Kegan Paul, 1956).

Berrington, H. (ed.) *Change in British Politics* (Case, 1983).

Bogdanor, V. *The People and the Party System* (Cambridge University Press, 1982).

Bogdanor, V. *Multi-Party Politics and the Constitution* (Cambridge University Press, 1983).

Butler, D. *The British General Election of 1951* (Macmillan, 1952).

Butler, D. *The British General Election of 1955* (Macmillan, 1955).

Butler, D. *The Electoral System in Britain since 1918*, 2nd edn (Oxford University Press, 1962).

Butler, D. and Butler G. *British Political Facts 1900–1985* (Macmillan, 1986).

Butler, D. and Kavanagh, D. *The British General Election of February 1974* (Macmillan, 1974).

Butler, D. and Kavanagh, D. *The British General Election of October 1974* (Macmillan, 1975).

Butler, D. and Kavanagh, D. *The British General Election of 1979* (Macmillan, 1980).

Butler, D. and Kavanagh, D. *The British General Election of 1983* (Macmillan, 1984).

Butler, D. and Kavanagh, D. *The British General Election of 1987* (Macmillan, 1988).

Butler, D. and Kavanagh, D. *The British General Election of 1992* (Macmillan, 1992).

Butler, D. and King, A. *The British General Election of 1964* (Macmillan, 1965).

Butler, D. and King, A. *The British General Election of 1966* (Macmillan, 1966).

Butler, D. and Pinto-Duschinsky, M. *The British General Election of 1970* (Macmillan, 1971).

Butler, D. and Ranney, A. *Electioneering* (Oxford, 1992).

Butler, D. and Rose, R. *The British General Election of 1959* (Macmillan, 1960).

Butler, D. and Stokes, D. *Political Change in Britain*, 2nd edn (Macmillan, 1974).

Cain, B., Ferejohn, J. and Fiorina, M. *The Personal Vote* (Harvard University Press, 1987).

Craig, F. *British Electoral Facts, 1832-1987* (1989).

Craig, F. *British Parliamentary Election Results 1950-70* (1971).

Craig, F. *Britain Votes 1974-79* (1980).

Craig, F. *Britain Votes 1983-87* (1988).

Crewe, I. and Harrop, M. *Political Communications: the British General Election of 1983* (Cambridge University Press, 1986).

Curtice, J. and Steed, M., 'Proportionality and exaggeration in the British electoral system', *Electoral Studies*, vol. 5 no. 3, Dec. 1986 pp. 209-28.

Dunleavy, P. and Husbands, C. *British Democracy at the Crossroads* (Allen & Unwin, 1985).

Finer, S. *The Changing British Party System 1945-1979* (American Enterprise Institute, 1980).

Finer, S. *Adversary Politics and Electoral Reform* (Anthony Wigram, 1975).

Franklin, M. *The Decline of Class Voting in Britain* (Oxford University Press, 1984).

Goodhart, C. and Bhansali, R. 'Political economy', *Political Studies*, vol. 18, no. 1, March 1970 pp. 43-106.

Gray, P. and Gee, F. *Electoral Registration for Parliamentary Elections* (OPCS, 1967).

Halsey, A. H. *Trends in British Society since 1900*, 2nd edn (Macmillan, 1988).

Hansard Society, *Agenda for Change* (Chataway Commission on election campaigns) (Hansard Society, 1991).

Heath, A. et al., *Understanding Political Change* (Pergamon, 1991).

Heath, A. et al., *Labour's Last Chance* (Dartmouth, 1994).

Heath, A., Jowell, R. and Curtice, J. *How Britain Votes* (Pergamon, 1985).

Hennessy, P. and Seldon, A. (eds) *Ruling Performance* (Basil Blackwell, 1987).

Himmelweit, H. *How Voters Decide* (Academic Press, 1985).

Johnston, R. *The Geography of English Politics* (Croom Helm, 1985).

Kavanagh, D. *Constituency Electioneering in Britain* (Longman, 1970).

Kavanagh, D. *Thatcherism and British Politics* (Oxford University Press, 1986).

King, A. (ed.), *Britain at the Polls 1992* (Chatham House, 1992).

McCallum, R. and Readman, A. *The British General Election of 1945* (Oxford University Press, 1947).

McKenzie, R. *British Political Parties*, 3rd edn (Heinemann, 1963).

McKenzie, R. and Silver, A. *Angels in Marble* (Heinemann, 1968).

Miller, W. *Electoral Dynamics in Britain since 1918* (Macmillan, 1977).

Milne, R. and Mackenzie, H. *Straight Fight* (Hansard Society, 1954).

Milne, R. and Mackenzie, H. *Marginal Seat* (Hansard Society, 1958).

Nicholas, H. *The British General Election of 1950* (Macmillan, 1951).

Penniman, H. *Britain at the Polls: the Parliamentary Elections of 1974* (American Enterprise Institute, 1975).

Penniman, H. *Britain at the Polls 1979* (American Enterprise Institute, 1981).

Penniman, H. and Ranney, A. *Britain at the Polls 1983* (American Enterprise Institute, 1985).

Pinto-Duschinsky, M. *British Political Finance 1830–1980* (American Enterprise Institute, 1982).

Robertson, D. *Class and the British Electorate* (Basil Blackwell, 1984).

Rose, R. *Do Parties Make a Difference?*, 2nd edn (Macmillan, 1984).

Rose, R. and McAllister, I. *Voters Begin to Choose* (Frances Pinter, 1986).

Särlvik, B. and Crewe, I. *Decade of Dealignment* (Cambridge University Press, 1983).

Seyd, P. and Whiteley, P., *Labour's Grass Roots* (Oxford University Press, 1992).

Seymour-Ure, C. *The Political Impact of the Mass Media* (Constable, 1974).

Teer, F. and Spence, J. *Political Opinion Polling* (Hutchinson, 1973).

Times House of Commons (published after each general election since 1929).

Todd, J. and Butcher, B. *Electoral Registration in 1981* (HMSO, 1982).

Waller, R. *The Almanac of British Politics*, 3rd edn (Croom Helm, 1987).

Worcester, R. and Harrop, M. *Political Communications: the General Election Campaign of 1979* (Macmillan, 1982).

Index

Abadan, 11
Action not Words, 24
addresses, 96–7, 110, 120
advertising, 17–18, 39, 88, 110–17
age and voting, 47, 61, 69
agents, 121
Aldermaston, 16
Alliance, 37, 38, 41, 42, 85, 91
Amery, J., 44
Angels in Marble, 73
Ashdown, P., 42
Attlee, Earl, 2, 5, 8, 11, 13, 15, 91,
    99
Avon, Earl of, 16, 75, 91, 99

balance of payments, 27
Balfour, Earl, 124
Ballot Act, 45
bandwagon effect, 119
Banff, 63
Barnes, Rosie, 59
Belfast, West, 37
Benney, M., 122
Benn, T., 21, 83, 125
Bermondsey, 37
Best Future for Britain, 42, 93
Better Tomorrow, A, 25
Bevan, A., 13, 15, 16, 117
Bevin, E., 11, 99
Bhansali, R., 73
bibliography, 135–6
black MPs, 81
black voters, 65, 69
Blackpool, 5, 9
Blair, T., 39

Blake, Lord, 58
Blyth, 80
Boothby, Lord, 11
Boundary Commission, 47, 49, 51–
    3
bribery, 45–6
Bristol, South, 66
Bristol, South-East, 48
Britain Belongs to You, 16
Britain Strong and Free, 31
Britain United, 40
Britain Will Win, 31, 40
British Airways, 38
British Broadcasting Corporation
    (BBC), 2, 106–8
British Coal, 42
British Electoral Behaviour, 74
British Oxygen, 21, 98
British Political Finance, 85
British Rail, 42
British Steel, 38
British Telecom, 38
Brittan, Sir L., 39
broadcasting, 2, 44, 49, 106–9
Brown, George, 21, 23–5
Brown, Gordon, 39
Budge, I., 101
Butler, R. A., 21
Butskellism, 9
by-elections, 19, 23, 29, 37, 39, 40

Caithness and Sutherland, 80
Callaghan, Lord, 22, 32–3, 36, 37,
    100
campaign duration, 77–8

Campaign for Nuclear
    Disarmament (CND), 16
campaigning, 90–101, 120–1
candidate's expenses, 86–8
candidates, 78, 81–3
canvassing, 120–1
carpet-bagging, 83
Carrington, Lord, 58
Castle, Barbara, 35
Chalker, Lynda, 43
Changing Britain for Good, 42
Chifley, B., 125
Churchill, Sir W., 2, 5, 8, 11–13, 14,
    20, 74, 91, 99
Clarke, K., 27
class, 67
communications, 2, 121
computerization, 121
conscription, 16
Conservative Manifesto, 1979, 35
Conservative Manifesto, 1983, 38
constituencies, 51–4
Corrupt Practices Act, 45–6
cost of elections, 85–8
counting of votes, 99
Crewe, I., 74
Cripps, Sir S., 11
Crosby, 37, 59
Crossman, R., 91
cube law, 54, 117
Curtice, J., 60, 67, 84

Daily Express, 15, 105, 115
Daily Mail, 10, 105
Daily Mirror, 7, 8, 11, 12, 102–3,
    105
Daily Sketch, 105, 115
Davies, C., 10
Davies, S. O., 80
de Gaulle, C., 21
Deakin, A., 88
declaration of results, 99–100
Dell, E., 35
deposits, 47, 78
deselection of MPs, 83
devolution, 32, 48
Devon West, 48
direct mail, 121
dissolution, 75–7

Douglas-Home, Sir A., 21, 23, 83,
    100
Downing St., 65, 100
duration of Parliament, 75–8

Economic Affairs, Dept. of, 23
Economist, 54
Eden, Sir A., 16, 74, 91, 99
education, 14, 65, 82–3
election
    addresses, 96–7, 110, 120
    expenses, 47, 86–8
    law, 45–50
    night, 99–100
    petitions, 48
    timetable, 75–6
Election Registers Act, 46
electoral system, 55–9
electorate, 52, 130
Elizabeth II, Queen, 100
Euro-elections, 42, 80
European Assembly Elections Act, 47
European Communities
    (Amendment) Act, 48
European Economic Community
    (EEC), 19, 25, 27, 28, 30, 38,
    87–8
European Parliament, 42, 47
Evans, G., 35
Everest, Mount, 14
Ewing, Winifred, 35
expenditure, 86–8, 114

Falklands war, 38, 123
Fermanagh and S. Tyrone, 48, 64
Figgures, Sir F., 29, 97
finance, 86–8
Firm Action for a Fair Britain, 29
Fisher, Sir H., 58
Five Year Plan, 5
Foot, M., 36–7, 39, 53, 83, 97
Foot et al. v. *Boundary Commission*, 49
forces vote, 5
Forward with Labour, 14
franchise, 61

Gaitskell, H., 16, 21, 91, 98
Gallup Poll, 8, 14, 31, 115
general election of 1880, 2; of 1918,
    97; of 1924, 97; of 1945, 5–7;

of 1950, 9–10; of 1951, 11–13;
of 1955, 14, 97; of 1959, 16–
19; of 1964, 19–23; of 1966,
23–5; of 1970, 25–7; of Feb.
1974, 27–30; of Oct. 1974, 30–
2; of 1979, 32–6; of 1983, 36–
8; of 1987, 38–41; of 1992,
41–5
Gerrymandering, 53
Gestapo, 5
Gilmour, Sir I., 43
Glasgow, 56
Goldwater, B., 124
Goodhart, C., 73
Gordon-Walker, Lord, 23
Gould, B., 35
Greater London Council (GLC), 38,
96
Greenwich, 40, 59
Green Party, 42
Grimond, Lord, 19

Hailsham, Vt., 21
Hansard Society, 58, 89
Hardy Spicer, 23
Harper et al. v. *Home Sec.*, 48
Harrison, M., 92
Healey, D., 43
Heath, E., 23, 31, 35, 69, 75
Heseltine, M., 3, 9, 23, 41
Hill, Lord, 11
Hogg, Q., 21
holiday voting, 47, 63
Home, E. of, 21, 23, 83
Houghton, Lord, 87
hours of voting *House of Commons
(Redistribution of Seats) Act
(1947)* 46; (1949) 116
House of Lords, 9
housing, 65, 97
How Britain Votes, 122
Howe, Sir G., 20, 23, 41, 43, 83
Howells, G., 44
Hudson, H., 108
Hull, 24

immigration, 69, 97, 99
In Place of Strife, 25
income of voters, 65
Independent Television Act, 47

Industrial Relations Act, 27
inflation, 23, 31, 36, 39
intimidation, 49
issues, 92–5
It's Time to Get Britain Working Again,
42, 93

Jenkins, Lord, 37, 38
Joseph, Lord, 18, 37

Kensington, North, 48
Kinnock, N., 2, 27, 39–40, 42, 108,
127
Kinross and S. Perth, 48
knocking-up, 120
Korean war, 11, 14, 123

Labour isn't Working, 113, 115
Labour Way is the Better Way, The, 35
Laski, H., 8
Let us Face the Future, 5
Let us Win through Together, 10, 93
Let us Work Together, 29
Liberal Party, 10, 11, 19, 21, 37, 72,
78, 81–2, 108
Life's Better with the Conservatives, 17,
18, 111
Lincoln, 80
Liverpool, 56, 67
Liverpool, Earl of, 41
Lloyd, S., 19
Lloyd George, Earl, 97
local campaigning, 120–1
London County Council (LCC), 11

McCallum, R., 59, 122
McKenzie, R., 73
Macleod, I., 21
MacManaway, J., 49
Macmillan, H., 16, 18, 19, 20, 83,
97, 107
Major, J., 35, 41, 129
Manchester, 67
mandate, 96
manifestos, 5, 92–5, 124
Market and Opinion Research
International (MORI), 117
Marshall v. *BBC*, 44
Maudling, R., 23
media, 102–9

meetings, 120–1
Members of Parliament, 81–4
Merthyr, 80
Mid-Ulster, 48
Milne, E., 80
Milne, R., 122
miners, 27, 30, 39, 81
Moore, J., 43
Morrison, Lord, 10, 18
Mr Cube, 11
Mussadiq, M., 11

Namier, Sir L., 122
National Health Service, 14, 40, 43, 97
National Plan, 25
nationalization, 5, 9, 14, 38, 97
Nationalists, 72
New Britain, The, 21
New Hope for Britain, 38
News Chronicle, 54
newspapers, 111–14
Next Five Years, The, 18
Next Moves Forward, The, 40
Norfolk, 14
North Sea oil, 126
Northern Ireland, 25, 30, 79, 123
Now Britain's Strong, 25, 37
nuclear weapons, 99

occupations of voters, 68–9
opinion polls, 8, 10, 30, 44, 115–18
Opinion Research Centre, 115, 117
Orpington, 8, 19
Owen, D., 2, 23, 39, 40, 42, 43, 91
Oxford, East, 66

Pardoe, J., 35, 91
Parker Smith, J., 54
Parkinson, C., 43
participation, 62–3, 131
Partisan Dealignment in Britain, 122
partisanship, 63–73
Patten, C., 35, 43, 44
Patten, J., 35
Paying for Politics, 89
personation, 49
Phillips, M., 18, 91
photo-opportunities, 2, 91, 107
Pinto-Duschinsky, M., 85

Plaid Cymru, 29, 80
Plant, Lord, 58
Political Change in Britain, 73, 122
Political Impact of the Mass Media, 102
poll tax, 41
polls, 8, 10, 30, 44, 54, 115–18
postal vote, 47, 63
posters, 110–11, 120
Powell, E., 21, 25, 27, 29, 37, 63, 69
Prescott, J., 27
press, 102–6, 111–12
press conferences, 91, 103
printing, 121
Prior, J., 18, 58
private polls, 117–18
privatization, 38, 42
Profumo, J., 21
proportional representation, 57–9
Prosperity with a Purpose, 21
psephology, 106, 122
Putting Britain First, 31
Pym, F., 20, 58

R. v. *Tronoh Mines*, 47
racism, 67
radio, 2, 106–8
Rae, N., 60
redistribution of seats, 11, 46–51
Redistribution of Seats Act (1947) 46, (1949) 51
Referendum Act, 47
referendums, 32, 34, 47, 87
regional factors, 67
register, 61–2, 120
religion, 69
Representation of the People Acts (1948) 46, 51; (1949) 45; (1958) 47; (1969) 47; (1981) 45; (1983) 45, 47; (1985) 47
Resale Price Maintenance, 21
Rhodesia, 123
Robertson, Sir D., 80
Rolls-Royce, 27
Romford, 51
Roosevelt, F. D., 99

Saatchi and Saatchi, 111
Salisbury, M. of, 16
Savings Bank scare, 97
scares, 97

Scotland, 26, 52–3, 67
Scottish Nationalists, 29, 36, 80
seats and votes, 55–9, 130–1
selection of candidates, 82–3
sex and voting, 69
Seymour-Ure, C., 102
Sheffield, 44
Shove, P., 20
Sillars, J., 44
Smith, J., 27
Smith, Sir C., 44
Smith Square, 91
snap elections, 75–6
Social Democratic Party (SDP), 37,
    40, 72, 79
Southwark, North, 51
Speaker's Conference, 48, 119
Stalin, J., 14, 99
Stansgate, Vt., 21
Steed, M., 60, 67, 84
Steel, D., 35, 37, 38, 91
Stewart, M., 35
Stockton, Earl of, 16, 18, 19, 20, 80,
    97, 107
Strauss, G., 35
Suez, 16, 123
Sun, 102–5
Supermac, 19
swing, 54–5

tactical voting, 60
Tate and Lyle, 11
Taverne, D., 80
taxation, 40, 43
Tebbit, N., 27, 43, 91
telephone owners, 65
television, 2, 106–9
Thatcher, Margaret, 2, 31, 32, 36,
    41, 43, 64, 73, 97, 123, 124
This is the Road, 10, 93
Thorneycroft, Lord, 16
Thorpe, J., 18, 29, 35
three-day week, 34, 39
Time for Decision, 24
Tonight, 107
trade union MPs, 81–2

transfer of power, 99–100
Transport and General Workers
    Union, 88
Tronoh Mines, 47, 112
turnout, 62–3, 130–1

U-turn, 27
underdog effect, 119
unemployment, 14, 39, 96
Unionists, 56
United for Peace and Progress, 14
university seats, 52
Upper Clyde, 27

Value Added Tax (VAT), 36
Vietnam, 25
volatility, 71
votes and seats, 55–9

Wales, 52–3
Walker, P., 43
Walworth Rd, 91
Wapping, 39
'Warmonger theme', 11, 12, 97
Wellington, Duke of, 3
Welsh Nationalists, 29, 80
Westland affair, 39
Whitelaw, Vt., 35
Williams, P., 84
Williams, Shirley, 20, 35, 37, 59
Wilson, Lord, 11, 21–32, 64, 75,
    100, 125
Wilson v. *IBA*, 49
window-bills, 110
winter of discontent, 32
Wolfe v. *IBA*, 49
women MPs, 81
Worcester, R., 117
Working Together for Britain, 38

Yom Kippur war, 29
You can Change the Face of Britain, 29
Younger, G., 20, 43

Zinoviev letter, 97